HOW TO LIVE A VICTORIOUS CHRISTIAN LIFE

*A Biblical Guide for
All Believers in Christ*

JOHN MARINELLI

How to Live a Victorious Christian Life: A Biblical Guide for All Believers in Christ
Copyright ©2021 by Rev. John Marinelli
All rights reserved.
First Edition: 2021

Print ISBN: 978-1087950167
eBook ISBN: 978-1087950174

Contact:
P. O. Box 831413
Ocala, FL. 34483

Cover and Formatting: Streetlight Graphics

No part of this book may be reproduced, scanned, or distributed in any printed or electronic form without permission. Please do not participate in or encourage piracy of copyrighted materials in violation of the author's rights. Thank you for respecting the hard work of this author.

TABLE OF CONTENTS

Preface v

Introduction vii

Chapter One 1

Chapter Two 17

Chapter Three 38

Chapter Four 51

Chapter Five 61

Chapter Six 72

Chapter Seven 78

Chapter Eight 88

Chapter Nine 101

Chapter Ten 111

Chapter Eleven 122

Chapter Twelve 130

Conclusion 139

About The Author 141

PREFACE

The author's purpose in writing, *"How To Live A Victorious Christian Life"* is to call attention to the possibility of living in victory in a society that has turned away from God and His righteousness. *"How do I do it on a daily basis?"* is discussed in detail.

Several Biblical promises will be revealed and discussed so as to lead the reader into the reality of assurance and faith.

The author's goal is to teach a simple "How To" methodology in walking by faith.

Scripture references will be use and marked with bible addresses for validation so as to satisfy the skeptical mind. In most cases the KJV will be used.

INTRODUCTION

Life can be very different for people in today's world. You can live life for yourself, or dedicate your life to helping others. You can work long hours or do no work at all.

Whatever lifestyle you live, it will come with its own set of rules and regulations. You will have to apply them to be successful. The Christian life is no different. You will have to learn and apply Bible truth.

The problem is, there are too many teachers, most of which are off base in their thinking. (My humble opinion) I'll bet you didn't know that there are over 3,000 different Christian denominations in existence today. Guess what? For the most part, they are all teaching different doctrines and telling their followers that they have to abide by their rules in order to have a successful or abundant Christian life. What it means to be a Christian has been lost over the centuries. Even in the 1st century it was confusing.

It's time to get back to the Bible and let it speak for itself. That's what this book is all about. My input is centered in Bible truths that you can use in every day life. Apply them and you will live a victorious Christian life as God intended it to be. It won't be man's expectations.

If you are anything like me, you need to be, "Fully Persuaded" before you commit to doing anything. It could be moving to another city, cutting back on coffee, marriage or a host of other life decisions. Living the Christian lifestyle in no different.

I have been a Christian for over 60-years and I must admit, if I want to be honest, that I have not always been fully persuaded. It has been an up and down ride, like a roll-a-coaster, as I stammered in my faith, fell into doubt and even walked away concluding that it was just too hard. I didn't have it in me to be a good Christian. I just kept failing God and disappointing myself.

All that changed when I realized that salvation was by Grace. The idea that salvation could be obtained through works was and still is a lie. I had made a false assumption.

I guess it was when the Holy Spirit spoke to my heart saying, "If man could have lived the life, never falling short of God's holiness, there would be no need for Jesus to die as a sacrifice or penalty for sin. There would be no sin. Think about it!"

Then I read in the scriptures, in the book of Romans, chapter three, *"For all have sinned, and come short of the glory of God." Romans 3:23*

Then it hit me, if all had sinned then all were guilty, not just me. All were in need of a savior including me. There were no perfect people, only sinners that needed God's forgiveness.

I realized that I knew very little about God and His plan for the ages. I needed to be educated, persuaded and assured that there was a way for me to realize the destiny that God wanted me to attain. Thus began my search to know God and His love. It was the only way I could know how to live the Christian Life. Here's what I discovered and offer to you.

CHAPTER ONE

Life's Most Important Questions

Most of us live our lives based upon assumptions that may or may not be true. Some folks don't even question the thought process that society says is the basis for living. There is no **"Real Truth"** anymore. It seems to be your truth or my truth but never **"Absolute Truth."** I guess that is why so many folks are confused and have difficulty trying to live a victorious Christian Life. The truth seems to elude them.

I believe that "Absolute Truth" comes from God and is revealed in the Bible. In order to know God's truth concerning our existence, we must ask ourselves three basic questions and look to the scriptures for the answers. Our conclusions will literally determine the way we live as Christians here on earth and what our eternal destiny will be. They are also the basis for our everyday perspectives.

Life's Most Important Questions:

- Where did I come from?
- Why am I here?
- What happens to me when I die?

We answer these questions based upon what we believe. Our Christian lifestyle is built on what we believe. Our actions are determined by how we think.

There is a Bible verse that illustrates my point. Hear what Jesus said.

"Everyone then who hears these words of mine and does them will be like a wise man who built his house on the rock. And the rain fell, and the floods came, and the winds blew and beat on that house, but it did not fall, because it had been founded on the rock."

"And everyone who hears these words of mine and does not do them will be like a foolish man who built his house on the sand. [27] And the rain fell, and the floods came, and the winds blew and beat against that house, and it fell, and great was the fall of it." **Matt. 7:24-27**

Knowing what God says is true and applying it will always keep us in times of trouble. So it is in this life. We must know the answers to life's most important questions and apply them in order to be fulfilled as a person. To do otherwise is a self-deception that will steal our destiny and condemn us to a life of heartache. We will miss all that God has for us.

The 1st question is
Where Did We Come From?

Over the past 60 years, we have been deceived into thinking that we came into existence as a result of evolution. (God's "Absolute Truth" was replaced by an ungodly theory.)

Evolution says there is no God and all that exist is a result of random selection. Some *"Think-tanks"* will acknowledge the existence of a god but will not ascribe any personality to it or active interaction with man.

It is true that various chemicals exist, however, that doesn't mean they can evolve, on their own, into any kind of life. That's like saying if I put the parts of a car in a garage and let them simmer for a million or billion years, they will evolve, on their own, into a fully operational vehicle.

Life is more than a mixture of chemicals. Random Selection cannot produce anything more than gobbledygook.

Man Is & Always Will Be A Special Creation of God

The Bible tells us that God created man. **That's where we came from.** Life does not make any sense unless we are God's special creation.

He formed man out of the dust of the ground and He breathed into him the breath of life, **which was His own life force, His own Spirit.** God's life caused man to become alive, a living soul.

Here's the supporting text. *"And the LORD God formed man of the dust of the ground, **and breathed into his nostrils** the breath of life; and man became a living soul."* **Genesis 2:7**

The very definition of life, from a Biblical perspective, is being joined spiritually with our creator. We must have His life in us to be alive. Those who do not have His "breath of life" dwelling in them are no more than the walking dead.

A Living Soul

The human soul is a combination of Mind, Will and Emotion. This is where we reason, make decisions and feel. The wonder of it all is seen in the fact that man can operate within his soul separate from God. He can exist and control his own destiny. The problem with that is…God never wanted man to exist separate from Him. His plan was that they walk together in perfect harmony.

God indwelled man and empowered him to live on a Godly plane of existence where he could be blessed and loved. True life is when man is indwelled with God's Spirit. This connects God with man and man with God. Man does not really live without God. He may exist but not as a living soul.

Being A Special Creation

If we are honest with each other, we can admit that there are many times that we do not feel special and wonder why it is that God created us. What's so special that we should marvel at our existence?

The difference between man and the rest of creation is that man was made in the image of God.

If we study the account of man's creation and his sin against his creator, we immediately realize that Adam lost the image and likeness of God when he sinned. Instead, he took on the very nature of evil. Let me show you from the scriptures.

Romans 5:12, 18 & 19

"Therefore, just as sin came into the world through one man, and death through sin, and so death spread to all men because all sinned" **Romans 5:12** (This is a reference to Adam's Original Sin)

"Therefore, as one trespass led to condemnation for all men, so

one act of righteousness leads to justification and life for all men."

"For as by the one man's disobedience, the many were made sinners, so by the one man's obedience, the many will be made righteous."

Sometimes the King James Version is hard to understand so just in case you are having trouble, here is the New Living Translation of the same text.

When Adam sinned, sin entered the world. Adam's sin brought death, so death spread to everyone, for everyone sinned.

Yes, Adam's one sin brings condemnation for everyone, but Christ's one act of righteousness brings a right relationship with God and new life for everyone.

Because one person disobeyed God, many became sinners. But because one other person obeyed God, many will be made righteous.

The above scriptures tell us that sin entered the world by and through the transgression of Adam, the first man. They also tell us that Adam's descendants took on the nature of sin. The, "breath of life" given by God was taken from Adam. He was cut off from God.

Adam's Transgression

When we transgress we go beyond the limits imposed upon us by law, command or other statute. Speeding is going beyond the legal limit imposed by law. So it was with Adam. He went beyond the command of God. The Bible calls it disobedience.

Adam decided to ignore God's command and do his own thing.

His rebellion led him into a realm void of God's love and grace. He became the lord over his own life and crowned himself as his own god.

This attitude became the basis of the *"Sin Nature"* that passed on to his descendants and is what rules our world today. It is a, **"Do Your Own Thing"** philosophy.

God never wanted Adam to know evil. His plan for mankind was only good. We were created by God so we could do His thing, not our own. His thing was our thing.

God's Thing

All the good, the blessings, the joys of life and our eternal destiny are wrapped up in ***"God's Thing."***

In **Genesis 2:17** God tells Adam regarding the tree of the knowledge of good and evil, "in the day that you eat from it you shall surely die."

The saying that Adam would die was a Spiritual death that occurred at the moment he ate from the tree? Adam physically died 930 years later.

This proves out as seen in future Biblical accounts where Adam no longer walked continually in God's Spirit. He instead encountered another nature in himself that was contrary to the will of God.

We can understand the sudden appearance of a new destructive nature in Adam by considering a pregnant girl that is a drug addict who has a baby while on drugs and discovers that her baby is also an addict. The drugs passed on to the child.

So it is with the sin nature. It was passed on from Adam to his descendants down through the ages. Thus, all are infected. All have sinned.

God's special creation was cut off from its creator and God's desire to fellowship on His level with man was lost. God lost the image of Himself in the earth and man lost his Spiritual bond with God.

But the story doesn't end here. There is more. It's called, "The Gospel" or " Good News"

Jesus came to earth to *seek and to save* that, which was lost. "For the Son of Man has come to seek and to save that which was lost." **Luke 19:10** The loss was the image and likeness of God that was placed into Adam.

So we, as the descendants of Adam, are a fallen race that is in need of redemption. However, God did not cast us off. He restored His image and likeness in man through the cross of Jesus Christ.

He paid the penalty for our sins and lived the life we should have lived before God. That's why He is our savior. That's why He is the only way to God. No other man could qualify because they are all of a fallen nature and in need of a savior.

Some folks reject the sacrificial death of Christ for the sins of mankind saying that He was also a descendant of Adam and therefore equally guilty of sin. However, they forget that *Jesus was born of a virgin.* He escaped the sin nature that was passed on to humanity through Adam. His unique birth qualified Him to become the spotless Lamb of God.

We are forgiven because Jesus died in our stead and we are accepted because Jesus never sinned. His righteousness is imputed into us and His blood cleanses us from all unrighteousness. It's as though we had never sinned. Listen to what Jesus said as recorded by the apostle John.

"For God so loved the world, that he gave his only begotten Son, that whosoever believeth in him should not perish, but have everlasting life" **John 3:16**

The Apostle John tells us, *"If we confess our sins, he is faithful and just to forgive us our sins, and to cleanse us from all unrighteousness."* **I John 1:9**

Once the blood of Jesus cleanses us from all sin and we are saved by His life, we can rest assured that indeed, we are a Special Creation of God.

Redeemed By The Blood of the Lamb Jesus Christ

Here's what the Apostle Paul said.

"That if thou shalt confess with thy mouth the Lord Jesus, and shalt believe in thine heart that God hath raised him from the dead, thou shalt be saved."

"For with the heart man believeth unto righteousness; and with the mouth confession is made unto salvation." **(Romans 10:9-10)**

Knowing this gives us selfworth, no matter who accuses us or tells us different.

We are His creation and His beloved. *"For we are his workmanship, created in Christ Jesus unto good works, which God hath before ordained that we should walk in them."* **Ephesians 2:10**

> It is God's Love for us that compels us to repent and be filled with his, "Breath of Life" to become a new Creature.
>
> No more "Walking Dead".

The 2nd question is Why Am I Here?

Some folks actually killed themselves because they could not figure out what life was all about.

Suicide… says that there is, "No Point To Life", "That we have no value as an individual", "That life has no meaning" ***Why Are We Here?***

Here are some Suicide statistics from the American Foundation For Suicide Prevention

While this data is the most accurate we have, we estimate the numbers to be higher. Stigma surrounding suicide leads to under-reporting, and data collection methods critical to suicide prevention need to be improved.

> Suicide is the 10th leading cause of death in the US.
>
> Each year, 42,773 Americans die by suicide

Additional Facts About Suicide in the US

The annual age-adjusted suicide rate is **12.93 per 100,000** individuals. Men die by suicide **3.5x** more often than women.

On average, there are **117** suicides per day. White males accounted for **7 of 10** suicides in 2014. Firearms account for **almost 50%** of all suicides. The rate of suicide is **highest in middle age** — white men in particular. Over 20 vetrans kill themselves every day. On average, 1 person commits suicide every 16-minutes. Untreated Depression is the #1 cause of suicide. There are 2 times as many deaths due to suicide than AIDS.

> For every suicide, there are 25 attempted Suicides at a costs of $44 Billion annually

Most adults are still searching for an identity, even into their senior years. They go through life holding on to titles as a way of explaining who they are. (Why they exist.)

The Used-To-Be Scenario

I live about 30 minutes north of The Villages, a huge retirement community. I know a lot of folks from that area. I hear some of them saying, "I used to be" or "I was" but rarely do I hear, "I AM". Some folks seem to have lost their identity and in the process of living life. More than 7,500 seniors took their own lives in 2014.

We were created in the image and likeness of God. Genesis 1:27 records the event,

"And God created man in his own image, in the image of God created he him; male and female created he them."

Here's what Jesus said about why He came to earth.

"The thief cometh to steal, and to kill, and to destroy: I am come that they might have life, and that they might have it more abundantly." **John 10:10**

We can live an abundant life. This is a life that is full of blessings, love and forgiveness. It is what Jesus wanted for us and made available to all who trust in Him.

A Purpose Driven Life

God had a purpose for us in His creation. We were not just a random selection without a reason to exist. It was and still is… to bear His image and likeness in the earth; to have dominion over every creature on the earth and to fellowship with God in the beauty of holiness.

God, being a Spirit, as the Bible tells us, says that the image and likeness of God is not a physical resemblance but rather Spiritual. He wanted us to be the embodiment of His character, which is …

"Love, Peace, Joy, Longsuffering, Meekness, Gentleness, Self-Control, Goodness and Faith." **Galatians 5:22-23**

Unfortunately, we see more anger, hate, murder, jealousy, and evil flowing from the hearts of our fellowman. When abortion is deemed a health issue instead of murder, we know that the image of God has been lost.

Over **60 million** babies have been killed in the womb since the Rowe vs. Wade Supreme Court decision. This is not what God intended. We were not created to kill our unborn in the name of good health.

We were created by God to show forth His glory and to have fellowship with Him. He is the only true and living God. What we do in life, as to a profession, should not exclude God. We are, after all, His image and likeness.

We can reflect God's glory as workers, retirees, housewives, children or whatever we desire to do or be… as long as our light is shining bright with the Love of God. *This is why we were placed upon this earth at this moment in time.* This is the abundant life.

The 3rd question is, Where Are We Going When We Die?

Do you remember the story when Jesus was telling His disciples that He was going away? (Referring to His death on the cross) Here's the account.

Simon Peter said unto him, Lord, where goest thou? Jesus answered him, where I go, thou canst not follow me now; but thou shalt follow me afterwards. Peter said unto him, Lord, why cannot I follow thee now? I will lay down my life for thy sake. **John 13:36-37** Later He would tell Phillip,

"I am the way, the truth, and the life: no man cometh unto the Father, but by me." **John 14:6**

All roads did not lead to Rome, nor do all religions lead us to eternal life.

… Paul said,

"Neither is there salvation in any other: for there is none other

name under heaven given among men, whereby we must be saved." Acts 4:2

Do not think that you can get into heaven through a church, a religious leader, a set of rules and regulations, or a doctrine that is contrary to what the apostles taught? Hear what the apostle Paul said to the Corinthian church. I have amplified it to clarify its meaning. This is my interpretation based upon many other accepted versions.

"For if anyone comes to you preaching another Jesus, whom we, (The Apostles), have not preached, or if you receive another spirit, which is not the Holy Spirit that you have already received, or another gospel, which is different from what we taught you and you have already accepted, you will be deceived and end up accepting the teachings of that person who is really a false teacher." **II Corinthians 11:4**

> **Note**: The inference is that they should immediately reject such a person as a liar and false teacher. Those that follow such teachers will also suffer the judgment ascribed to them by God.

Our Future Home

"In my Father's house are many mansions: if it were not so, I would have told you. I go to prepare a place for you. And if I go and prepare a place for you, I will come again, and receive you unto myself; that where I am, there ye may be also." John 14:2-3

Jesus is the only way to God, the Father and He is even now engaged in the preparation of an eternal dwelling place for those who believe in him.

The Promise of God To The "Whosoevers" of This World

"For God so loved the world, that he gave his only begotten Son, that whosoever believeth in him should not perish, but have everlasting life." **John 3:16**

I decided long ago that I was one of those, *"Whosoevers"* and I did what Jesus said in **John 3:16.** I believed in Jesus as the only begotten Son of God. I believed that Jesus was indeed the only way to God the Father, who created me.

I believed that Jesus came to earth to die for my sins so I could have victory over death, hell and the grave. I believed that Jesus rose from the dead on the 3rd day as the scriptures declare.

I believed that He is preparing a place for me with Him in heaven. I am spending my senior years looking for my Savior to return and take me to my new home.

I am doing just fine, **but… what about you?** I want to invite you, "All of You" that read this book, to come into a saving knowledge of Jesus Christ. If you are not filled with the image and likeness of God, your creator, you need to be. He will recreate you if you ask Him. This is the 1st step in living a victorious Christian life. You must be "Born Again."

You can know the joy of being saved, of walking with God in this life and being assured of life after death when your time comes.

Hebrews 9:27 says, "And as it is appointed unto men once to die, but after this the judgment"

Please join me in being a **"Whosoever"** of **John 3:16** and discovering the joy of being saved. He will never let you down.

"Where Are You Going When You Die?"

There is only one true answer that brings abundant life here on earth and happiness in eternity. That answer is...*we will be with Jesus*. See it for yourself in the scriptures.

2-Corinthians 5:1-8

"For we know that if our earthly house of this tabernacle were dissolved, we have a building of God, an house not made with hands, eternal in the heavens. For in this we groan, earnestly desiring to be clothed upon with our house, which is from heaven:"

"If so be that being clothed we shall not be found naked. For we that are in this tabernacle do groan, being burdened: not for that we would be unclothed, but clothed upon, that mortality might be swallowed up of life."

"Now he that hath wrought us for the selfsame thing is God, who also hath given unto us the earnest of the Spirit. Therefore we are always confident, knowing that, while we are at home in the body, we are absent from the Lord: (For we walk by faith, not by sight:)"

"We are confident, I say, and willing rather to be absent from the body, and to be present with the Lord."

The point of chapter one is to fully persuade you that God is for you, not against you.

"I AM" THERE

"I AM" There,
At the end of your broken dreams,
Before the sun rises over your day,
Prior to those tear-filled streams.

"I AM" There,
Down that road of despair,
When all seems to be lost,
And no one seems to care.

"I AM" There,
Over all of life's twists and turns,
When tomorrow is all but gone,
And when you are full of concerns.

"I AM" There,
Sayeth the Lord of Host,
To bring you hope and peace,
And the power of my Holy Ghost.

"I AM" There,
To be sure you make it through,
In the midst of every trial,
To bless your life and deliver you.

"I AM" There
Written By John Marinelli

CHAPTER TWO

Knowing God's Will

When I was a young Christian, I wished with all my heart that I could actually know the will of God. I often sent up prayers to heaven saying, "Lord, what do I do now?" It got so bad that I could hardly drive my car because I couldn't decide if God wanted me in the left or right lane.

Months went by with my continual prayers to God that shouted into heaven, "What Do I Do Now?" Finally, I was invited to a Bible study, started going to church and began reading my Bible. The answers came ever so slow but fast enough for me to digest and store them away in my heart.

Now, after 60+ years of Bible study, prayer and life-application, I can say with confidence that I do know and understand God's Will. I am still learning and studying and applying. I even, at times, ask my self, "Why didn't I see that before now?"

I am going to open your eyes if you are blind, refresh your spirit if it is weary and strengthen your personal walk with Jesus, our Savior, by providing the tools needed to keep you keeping on. **Hang on!** It's sure to be an exciting adventure. This is part of living the Christian Life.

Knowing That You Know

If you call yourself a "Child of God", you should agree with me that you ought to know the Will of your Heavenly Father. You are openly admitting to a relationship and claiming family rights and access. **Are we in agreement so far?**

Knowing God is a logical assumption when we claim to be His child. Yet most of the Christians I know have serious doubts about the "Will of God" for them. This can only mean one of two things:

> ***Their relationship with God the Father is not a close one.*** They pray but never seek to hear from God. *or...*
>
> ***They have claimed to be a child of God but really are not.*** They know there is something not right but are too ashamed or afraid to openly admit to not being saved.

In either case, there is a way to *"know that you know"* so there is no more doubt. However, knowing that you know takes faith. God is speaking all the time through the Bible, through His Holy Spirit and through other folks that He brings into your life. The quick fix to *"Knowing That You Know"* is to *"Listen And Believe."*

I can say, without a doubt, that I know the Will of God for my life. I can make such a claim because God, my Heavenly Father, has published 66 books that contain over 7,000 promises and many great statements as to what His will is for His children. It's all there in the Bible, just waiting for us to dig them out, *"Listen and believe."*

To know that you know is a great feeling because there is no more anxiety. I know and have been persuaded that this way is the right way and my new perspective brings me a lot of comfort, peace and hope for the future.

"And thine ears shall hear a word behind thee, saying, this is the way, walk ye in it, when ye turn to the right hand, and when ye turn to the left." Isaiah 30:21

The Bible says, "For ye have not received the spirit of bondage again to fear; but ye have received the Spirit of adoption, whereby we cry, **Abba or Father**. The Spirit itself bears witness with our spirit, that we are the children of God: And if children, then heirs; heirs of God, and joint-heirs with Christ; if so be that we suffer with him, that we may be also glorified together." Romans 8:15-17

As the scripture says, the Spirit of God will bear witness with our spirits that we are the children of God. If you've ever felt, seen or otherwise realized the witness of God's Spirit, you will know without a shadow of a doubt, that you are a child of God.... and if a child also a joint heir with Christ.

How Does The Holy Spirit Bear Witness With Our Spirit?

Notice that the apostle Paul didn't say that the Spirit bears witness with our flesh, our souls or minds. He didn't say the witness would be through the intellect. He said the witness would be from **Spirit to spirit**. That means it could be one of many gentle quiet assurances that we did the right thing at the right time. It could be a sense of stability when things are going rough. It could be, an "I just know" feeling.

The point here is that God's Spirit is talking to us and our spirit is listening and rejoicing that it can hear God when He speaks. One definite witness, that I can recall, is when I read the scriptures. They started jumping off the page with new and fresh revelation. The Bible, all of a sudden, came alive and spoke directly to my spirit. God's Holy Spirit was and is still confirming to me that I am a child of the Living God.

So, we have a quiet assurance and a loud voice that calls us to the Word of God, where we receive faith, instruction, strength, knowledge and a lot more. God's witness is everywhere.

It's Not Rocket Science

Finding God's Will is not rocket science. We have already learned that God's Holy Spirit is available to confirm or excuse our decisions in life. We also know that it is our, "Free Will" that engages truth and activates faith to empower us to walk in the Spirit.

The key to **"Knowing That You Know"** is absolute submission to His Will. Here's what Jesus said, "If any man will do his will, (God's Will), he shall know of the doctrine, whether it be of God, or whether I speak of myself." John 17:7

We have to be ready and willing to do His Will. When we are, we will know the doctrine or revelation knowledge necessary to accomplish the revealed Will of God.

Question! Why should God give us the knowledge of His Will if we are not willing or not ready to use it? That would be a waste of time and energy on God's part and He just doesn't operate that way.

He has, however, already revealed His Will in the pages of the Bible. If we really want to know, we can read and discover and learn and apply all that God has for us. So, let's look at the Bible?

I will take you on a journey so you can discover some of the great and precious promises that prove out what the Will of God is. We will look at several scriptures and discuss them.

God's Divine Will As Revealed In The Bible

"And God said, Let us make man in our image, after our likeness: and let them have dominion over the fish of the sea, and over the fowl of the air, and over the cattle, and over all the earth, and over every creeping thing that creeps upon the earth." Genesis 1:26

God wanted to create man, (Mankind as Male & Female). His divine will was to create us. He did that in His likeness and image. Then He gave us dominion over the earth and all its life forms.

What does this say to us? Simply this, we were not a mistake, after thought or freak mutation of nature that evolved over millions of years. We were a specific, deliberate design to accomplish the goals and objectives of God in the earth.

"And let them have dominion" Genesis 1:26 The word, "Them" is all of us. We were to rule as the "Head" and not the Tail.

Now, let's proceed on our journey to discover the revealed "Will of God."

Revelation #1…God's will for our lives is to take dominion over evil and live in such a way as to reveal the image and likeness of God.

Man Is Created Male & Female

Genesis 2:18-25 is the biblical record of God creating Woman as a help meet for Adam. *"And the LORD God said, It is not good* that the man should be alone; I will make him a helper suitable for him."

And Adam said, *"This is now bone of my bones, and flesh of my flesh: she shall be called Woman, because she was taken out of Man. Therefore shall a man leave his father and his mother, and shall cleave unto his wife: and they shall be one flesh. And they were both naked, the man and his wife, and were not ashamed."*

Revelation #2... *It is God's Will for a man to have a woman at his side.* God ordained marriage and joined them together. Where does this leave Homosexuality? It was never in the will of God.

Revelation #3... *God's greatest creation, (Mankind), fell into sin and is now in need of a Savior.*

The Fall of Man

Death In Adam & Life In Christ

(Genesis 3:1-7; Genesis 7:1-5; 2 Peter 3:1-9)

Man falls from God's reality into the darkness of sin. He lost the image and likeness of God; But God still loves him and has a plan for his restoration. The blood of Jesus justifies man and His, (God's) righteousness is imparted to all who believe.

Revelation #4...God loves us & does not want us to perish. Jesus said, *"For God so loved the world, that he gave his only begotten Son, that whosoever believeth in him should not perish, but have everlasting life."* John 3:16 **The, "Whosoever" believers are given eternal life.**

"The Lord is not slack concerning his promise, as some men count slackness; but is longsuffering to us-ward, not willing that any should perish, but that all should come to repentance." II Peter 2:9

We must repent of our sin because Salvation is essential to knowing God's Will.

Revelation #5...God wants us to repent and accept Jesus as our Savior so we can live in relationship with Him.

"But God commended his love toward us, in that, while we were yet sinners, Christ died for us." Romans 5:8

He died for us that we might live for Him. (This is the foundation of the Gospel of Jesus Christ.)

Revelation #6...*God wants us to live life with a thankful heart.* This allows God to be God over us and allows us to expresses our dependence upon Him. It also relieves us from the burden and stress of being our own god. We don't have to be in control of everything.

Give Thanks In Everything

"In every thing give thanks: for this is the will of God in Christ Jesus concerning you." I Thessalonians 5:17

The Bible is filled with commands to give thanks to God (Psalm 106:1; 107:1; 118:1; 1 Chronicles 16:34; 1 Thessalonians 5:18).

Most verses go on to list reasons why we should thank Him, such as "His love endures forever" (Psalm 136:3), "He is good" (Psalm 118:29), and "His mercy is everlasting" (Psalm 100:5). Thanksgiving and praise always go together. We cannot adequately praise and worship God without also being thankful.

Feeling and expressing appreciation is good for us. Like any wise father, God wants us to learn to be thankful for all the gifts He has given us (James 1:17). It is in our best interest to be reminded that everything we have is a gift from Him.

Without gratefulness, we become arrogant and self-centered. We begin to believe that we have achieved everything on our own. Thankfulness keeps our hearts in right relationship to God, the giver of all good gifts. (Excerpts from www.gotquestions.org")

Revelation #7…God is worthy of our trust and when we trust in, rely upon and adhere to His voice, He will direct our paths.

Proverbs 3:5-6 offers another "Will of God" Revelation.

"Trust in the Lord with all thine heart; and lean not unto thine own understanding. In all thy ways acknowledge him, and he shall direct thy paths."

Why should we trust the Lord? Many Christians ask that question because of adverse situations they are in or have gone through. Here are a few reasons:

God is not a liar. He will always deal with us from a point of truth.

God is immutable, which means, He can never change. He does not say one thing and do another. When He speaks… Well, listen to how Isaiah put it. He is speaking for God…

"So shall my word be that goes forth out of my mouth: it shall not return unto me void, but it shall accomplish that which I please, and it shall prosper in the thing whereto I sent it." Isaiah 55:11

God is Love… This can only mean that He has no hate in him. His war and revenge is against His enemies who walk in darkness, steal, kill and destroy. His children are the *"Apple of His Eye"* and the subject of His grace.

God is our Protector…"The angel of the LORD encamps round about them that fear him, and delivers them." Psalm 34:7

God really does care for us... *"Casting all your care upon him; for he cares for you."* I Peter 5:7

"Cast thy burden upon the LORD, and he shall sustain thee: he shall never suffer the righteous to be moved." Psalm 55:22

God is a God of Blessings, Not Curses... (Psalms 1:1-3)

"Blessed is the man who walks not in the counsel of the ungodly, nor stands in the path of sinners, nor sits in the seat of the scornful; But his delight is in the law of the LORD, And in His law he meditates day and night. He shall be like a tree planted by the rivers of water, that brings forth its fruit in its season, whose leaf also shall not wither; and whatever he does shall prosper."

God is a God of Peace....

"And the God of peace shall bruise Satan under your feet shortly. The grace of our Lord Jesus Christ be with you. Amen." Romans 16:20

Because of who He is, we can, with confidence, acknowledge Him, trust Him, disregard our own feelings and follow His lead. He will always direct our paths.

Revelation #8...God's highest will is to bring us back to where He had originally intended us to be, in His Image. Thus He speaks through the pages of the Bible, letting us know that He wants us to set ourselves apart for fellowship with Him.

"For this is the will of God, even your sanctification, that ye should abstain from fornication:" I Thessalonians 4:3

The generic meaning of sanctification is "the state of proper functioning." To sanctify someone or something is to set that person or thing apart for the use intended by its designer. A pen is "sanctified" when used to write. Eyeglasses are "sanctified" when used to improve sight. In the theological sense, things are sanctified when they are used for the purpose God intended.

To sanctify, therefore, means, "to make holy." In one sense, only God is holy (Isaiah 6:3). God is separate, distinct, and there is no other. No human being or thing shares the holiness of God's essential nature.

The imperfect state of creation is a reminder that God's fully sanctified purpose for it has been disrupted by sin. Evil is the deprivation of the good that God intended for the creation He designed. The creation groans, awaiting its sanctification when everything will be set right (Romans 8:21-22 ; Rev. 20-21).

Human beings, made in God's image, were the pinnacle and focus of his creation. The sanctification of human beings, therefore, is the highest goal of God's work in the universe. God explicitly declared it to be His will (1 Thess 4:3).

He purposed that human beings be "like Him" in a way no other created thing is. Human beings are like God in their stewardship over creation (Gen 1:26-31).

We can never be holy in ourselves as He is Holy but by faith, we can become the very righteousness of God in Jesus Christ.

"For he hath made him to be sin for us, who knew no sin; that we might be made the righteousness of God in him." II Corinthians 5:21

Revelation #9… God wants us to allow the mind of Christ to be in us and to join Him in humility, and servitude so He can highly exalt us with Christ.

"Let this mind be in you which was also in Christ Jesus, who, being in the form of God, did not consider it robbery to be equal with God, but made Himself of no reputation, taking the form of a bondservant, and coming in the likeness of men.

"And being found in appearance as a man, He humbled Himself and became obedient to the point of death, even the death of the cross. Therefore God also has highly exalted Him and given Him the name, which is above every name, that at the name of Jesus every knee should bow, of those in heaven, and of those on earth, and of those under the earth, and that every tongue should confess that Jesus Christ is Lord, to the glory of God the Father." Philippians 2:5-11

Revelation #10...*God wants His Peace to Rule or referee in our hearts.*

"And let the peace of God rule in your hearts, to the which also ye are called in one body; and be ye thankful." Colossians 3:15

The word "Rule" in verse 15 actually expresses the intent to "Reign". It also can be interpreted as Referee as in a game. Paul is telling the church to allow the peace of God to referee any and all situations as though they were a game. By doing so, you can use God's peace as a referee's whistle. It will blow with anxiety, confusion, worry and so on to let you know that you are off sides and in need of a reconnect with the Holy Spirit to attain His peace and sustain an attitude of thankfulness.

If you find yourself in anger, worry or any other such attitude, you can automatically know that you have lost God's peace. God wants you to walk and live in His peace so you do not have to experience all that jazz of the flesh. It will kill you if left unattended.

Revelation #11...*God wants us to prove what is the good, and perfect will of God.*

"And be not conformed to this world: but be ye transformed by

the renewing of your mind, that ye may prove what is that good, and acceptable, and perfect, will of God." Romans 12:1

We cannot allow non-believers to define what is or is not the acceptable or perfect Will of God. We need to be the Bible that they will never read. We need to demonstrate what good is and what perfect is so others around us can see what the perfect will of God is. The only way to get the job done is to reject the pull of this world into all its sin and be transformed in our minds so we do not fall for the wiles of the devil.

How do we renew our minds? By transforming your own mind from always thinking evil to allowing the mind of Christ to dwell in you. He will do the rest. Your mission is to not be conformed to this world but to align yourself with God's Will.

Revelation #12… God wants us to put on the whole armor of God so the devil can't hurt us.

"Finally, my brethren, be strong in the Lord, and in the power of his might. Put on the whole armor of God, that ye may be able to stand against the wiles of the devil. For we wrestle not against flesh and blood, but against principalities, against powers, against the rulers of the darkness of this world, against spiritual wickedness in high places. Wherefore take unto you the whole armor of God, that ye may be able to withstand in the evil day, and having done all, to stand." Ephesians 6:10-13

Our fight is with the rulers of darkness. We are fighting because we need to defend ourselves. If we don't, we will become open game for the devil. Hear what Peter says in I Peter 5:8-9,

"Be sober, be vigilant; because your adversary the devil, as a roaring lion, walks about, seeking whom he may devour: Whom resist stedfast in the faith, knowing that the same afflictions are accomplished in your brethren that are in the world."

Revelation #13...*God Wants Us to Guard our Hearts With All Diligence.*

"Keep your heart with all diligence; for out of it are the issues of life." **Proverbs 4:23**

To keep ones heart is to guard it with all diligence. It implies that we should act as a gatekeeper that allows good things in and bad things from getting in. God wants us to protect our spiritual growth and resources. They can be depleted and even stolen by the devil.

Revelation #14...*God Wants Us to Pray Without Ceasing*

"Rejoice always, pray without ceasing, give thanks in all circumstances; for this is the will of God in Christ Jesus for you." I Thessalonians 5:16-18

We pray without ceasing when we start our day talking to God and maintain an atmosphere of prayer all day. We rejoice and give thanks along the way and life flows along like a calm gentle sea. We do not give thanks for every bad thing.

We give thanks *in* everything not *for* everything. There is a difference. The word, "FOR," in this context, means be happy that God sent this bad thing your way. The word, "IN," means give thanks that God is with you in this bad situation because He will help you to get out of it or go through it.

Revelation #15...God Wants Us To Have *Fellowship With Him.*

Fellowship With God

"That which was from the beginning, which we have heard, which we have seen with our eyes, which we have looked upon, and our hands have handled, of the Word of life;" I John 1:1

This simple and bold statement means that one can have a relationship with God. This idea would surprise many of the apostle John's readers, and it should be astounding to us. The Greek mind-set highly prized the idea of *fellowship*, but restricted it to men only - the idea of such an intimate relationship with God was revolutionary.

Jesus started the same kind of revolution among the Jews when He invited men to address God as *Father* (Matthew 6:9). We really can have a living, breathing relationship with God the Father, and with Jesus Christ. He can be, not only our Savior, but also our counselor and our closest friend.

Actually, for many people, this is totally unappealing. Sometimes it is because they don't know who God is, and an invitation to a personal relationship with God is about as attractive to them as telling an eighth-grader they can have a personal relationship with the school principal. But when we know the greatness, the goodness, and the glory of God, we want to have a relationship with Him.

Other people turn from this relationship with God because they feel so distant from Him. They want a relationship with God, but feel so disqualified.

John identified this eternally existent being, who was physically present with John and others as **the Word of Life**, as the same *Logos* spoken of in John 1:1.

The idea of the *Logos* - of the **Word** - was important for John and for the Greek and Jewish worlds of his day. For the Jew, God was often referred to as *the Word* because they knew God perfectly revealed Himself in His Word. For the Greek, their philosophers had spoken for centuries about the *Logos* - the basis for organization and intelligence in the universe, the ultimate reason that controls all things.

It is as if John said to everyone, "This *Logos* you have been talking about and writing about for centuries - well, we have heard Him, seen Him, studied Him, and touched Him. Let me now tell you about Him." (Excerpts from *David Guzik article on Fellowship With God*)

Revelation #16...*God Wants Us To Seek His Kingdom First, Above All Else.*

"But seek ye first the kingdom of God, and his righteousness; and all these things shall be added unto you." Matthew 6:33

Jesus said to seek first the kingdom of God in His Sermon on the Mount (Matthew 6:33). The verse's meaning is as direct as it sounds. We are to seek the things of God as a priority over the things of the world. Primarily, it means we are to seek the salvation that is inherent in the kingdom of God because it is of greater value than all the world's riches.

But how do we know if we're truly seeking God's kingdom first? There are questions we can ask ourselves. "Where do I primarily spend my energies? Is all my time and money spent on goods and activities that will certainly perish, or in the services of God—the results of which live on for eternity?"

Believers who have learned to truly put God first may then rest in this holy dynamic: "…and all these things will be given to you as well."

God has promised to provide for His own, supplying every need (Philippians 4:19), but His idea of what we need is often different from ours, and His timing will only occasionally meet our expectations.

A growing number of false teachers are gathering followers under the message "God wants you to be rich!" But that philosophy is not the counsel of the Bible. It is certainly not the counsel of Matthew 6:33, which is not a formula for gaining wealth.

It is a description of how God works. Jesus taught that our focus should be away from this world—its status and its lying allurements—and placed upon the things of God's kingdom. (Excerpts from gotquestions.org)

Matthew 6:33 is a call to priorities. We are invited to have fellowship with Christ but not in the appetites of sinful flesh. He wants us to walk with Him in His kingdom.

Jesus says that if we sell out to Him, He will provide for us but if our selling out is to get rich, we have missed it before we start. God certainly wants us to prosper and be in good health but not by manipulation or exultation of self.

Revelation #17…*God wants us to be filled with His Holy Spirit.*

"And be not drunk with wine, wherein is excess; but be filled with the Spirit; Speaking to yourselves in psalms and hymns and spiritual songs, singing and making melody in your heart to the Lord;" Ephesians 5:18-19

This scripture clearly reveals God's Will for His Followers: Don't get drunk, Be Filled and Sing. I want to focus more closely on being filled with the Spirit. I am sure you will agree that he is not referring to the spirit of evil or the human spirit of which we are already absorbed. It is obvious that the Spirit we need to be filled with is none other than the Spirit of the Lord.

How does one get filled with God's Spirit? The text here uses Greek words that mean to be continually filled as though it were possible to use up the Spirit and find yourself to be empty. I think that many Christians are running on empty and are in serious need of a fill-up.

Paul wrote: *"Do not get drunk on wine, which leads to debauchery. Instead, be filled with the Spirit."* In the original Greek, the phrase "be filled: is a present-tense verb".

To signify a "one-time filling," Paul would have used the past tense or a future verb tense; instead, he chose the present tense to denote that the filling of the Holy Spirit is not a one-time event, but a continual experience. Scripture says that we must be continually filled with the Spirit, not just once or twice.

The word filling seems awkward when referring to the Holy Spirit's entrance into our lives. The Spirit of God is not a liquid, like water. He does not fill a person the way cold milk fills a cup.

The Holy Spirit is God—He is one in essence with the Father and the Son—but He is also a distinct personality and has all the attributes thereof. That is why we refer to the Holy Spirit as the third person of the Trinity. Many Scripture passages point to these facts.

Like a person, the Holy Spirit searches, helps and guides. He knows; He feels; He wills. Scripture speaks of the Holy Spirit's mind, His love and His instruction. In **Ephesians 4:30**, Paul wrote: *"Do not grieve the Holy Spirit of God, with whom you were sealed for the day of redemption."*

The only way we can grieve someone is if the one we are grieving has feelings.

Because the Holy Spirit is a personality, it makes more sense to talk about the Holy Spirit's control or compulsion in our lives, rather than His filling of our lives. Holy Spirit-driven is a good way to look at our response to His control.

The Spirit—driven in a gentle, loving way, drives a person who is filled with the Spirit. A Spirit-driven person allows the Holy Spirit to direct and guide every decision.

Because the world, the flesh and the devil oppose the Spirit-controlled lifestyle, we need to be filled and renewed continually. (Excerpts taken from Joel Comiskey's article CBN.org.)

Baptism with the Holy Spirit or in the Holy Spirit in Christian theology is a term describing baptism (washing or immersion) in or with the Spirit of God and is frequently associated with the bestowal of spiritual gifts and empowerment for Christian ministry. (Acts 1:5,8)

To illustrate, consider this…if we drank water from a glass, then the water would be inside us. However, if we went to the beach and stepped into the ocean, then we would be in the water. We receive, as it were, a drink of the Holy Spirit when we are saved, but when we are baptized in the Spirit; it is as if that initial drink becomes an ocean that completely surrounds us.

Just as the indwelling Spirit that Christians receive when they are saved reproduces *the life* of Jesus, so the outpoured, or baptizing, Spirit reproduces *the ministry* of Jesus, including miracles and healings.

When Jesus gave the Great Commission (Matthew 28:19-20), He knew that His disciples could not fulfill it in their own power. Therefore, He had a special gift in store for them: It was His plan to give them the same power that He had -- the power of the Spirit of God. So, immediately after giving them the Great Commission,

Jesus commanded his disciples not to leave Jerusalem, but to wait for what the Father promised, "which," He said, "you heard of from Me; for John baptized with water, but you shall be baptized with the Holy Spirit not many days from now" **(Acts 1:4-5).** He further promised: "You shall receive power after that the Holy Spirit has come upon you; and you shall be My witnesses both in Jerusalem, and in all Judea and Samaria, and even to the uttermost part of the earth" (Acts 1:8).

The disciples waited in Jerusalem as Jesus had commanded, and one day when they were all together, *"suddenly there came from heaven a noise like a violent, rushing wind, and it filled the whole house where they were sitting. And there appeared to them tongues as of fire distributing themselves, and they rested on each one of them. And they were filled with the Holy Spirit and began to speak with other tongues, as the Spirit was giving them utterance"* (Acts 2:3,4).

Then Peter explained to the crowd that gathered around that they were seeing the working of God's Spirit and told them about Jesus. The Christian church began that day with the disciples and the three thousand people who joined them as a result of the day's events.

We can undertake making disciples of all nations with some degree of success without the baptism in the Holy Spirit, but when we do, we are undertaking a supernatural task with limited power.

It is God's will -- it is His commandment -- that we be baptized with and continually filled with the Holy Spirit: ***"Be filled with the Spirit"*** (Ephesians 5:18). The knowledge and reality of the empowering Spirit enables us to reproduce the works of Jesus. (Excerpts from CBN.org)

So, as I see it, the baptism of the Spirit is given so the believer can receive ministry gifts to aid in his or her service to the Lord. The In-filling of the Spirit is to replenish the refreshing required to continue day to day. One has to do with reaching out to others. The other has to do with hearing and fellowshipping with God so we have direction, purpose and a clear focus.

Revelation #18... *God Wants Us to Know That He Is Working Everything Together For Good.*

Why should we Trust God, Give Thanks, Pray Without Ceasing, and follow all the other teachings? I would venture to say because of Romans 8:28,

"And we know that all things work together for good to them that love God, to them who are the called according to his purpose."

God's Will is clearly revealed but only accomplished in the lives of those that Love God and are the called according to His purposes. We also know that God calls everyone to repentance and salvation (John 3:16). The next pre-qualifier is that we love God.

You would think that His children would love their father. If they do not, it's because they do not know Him. In any event, loving God is the prime directive. Jesus said,

"And thou shalt love the Lord thy God with all thy heart, and with all thy soul, and with all thy mind, and with all thy strength: this is the first commandment." Mark 12:30

I am sure you will see even more scriptures that will reveal the "Will of God" for your life as you keep reading the Bible. I have listed some more prominent ones so you can get a feel for what to look for as you read.

So far, we have discovered 18 scriptures that should be active in our lives today. These revelation truths are more than enough to fully persuade a serious God-seeker that His will is centered on us and our destiny is in Him.

The best way to know God's Will is to ask God in prayer, stay in the Bible and look for direction, correction and guidance. ***It's all there.*** If you start a log of scripture verses and what they specifically meant to you, you'll have a history to refer to when you feel lost or confused.

The Best way to live a victorious Christian life in this world is to apply the scriptures and live in them moment by moment. The truth you find in the scriptures will far exceed what this world has to offer. If you can do this, you will become fully persuaded that God is able and willing to be with you in every life situation.

CHAPTER THREE

Knowing Who You Are In Christ

You cannot live a victorious Christian life if you do not know who you are in Christ. The biggest and most powerful lie that Satan uses to defeat the church of Jesus Christ is, "you do not have the authority to take charge and rule over evil forces."

The devil keeps telling us that when Jesus ascended after his resurrection He left us powerless.

The lie that has persisted in Christian circles and has become a dogma is that all that miracle working power ended with the death of the apostles. This heresy is now commonplace and believed by most evangelicals.

Do you have power from on high to overcome evil by casting out demons, healing the sick, binding Satan from your thoughts or changing the outcome of a circumstance? Most folks are afraid to even try. They shy away from seeking the Lord for a Word of Wisdom or a Word of Knowledge that would help them to better know and accomplish God's Will.

Do you read the Bible, as it were, a history book? Or is it alive with revelation and truth that stirs up your faith and builds your confidence to act upon what is being communicated?

What if I told you that you have authority as a believer? The same authority that Jesus had and still has is yours. All you need is to engage your free will and receive it.

You can become the head and not the tail.

"And the LORD shall make thee the head, and not the tail; and thou shalt be above only, and thou shalt not be beneath; if that thou hearken unto the commandments of the LORD thy God, which I command thee this day, to observe and to do them:" **Deut. 28:13**

You can live a victorious life. You just need to believe. How do I know, because Jesus said so?

"The thief cometh not, but for to steal, and to kill, and to destroy: I am come that they might have life, and they might have it more abundantly." **John 10:10**

The Source of
Your Authority

We can all agree, I think, that the source of our Spiritual authority comes from Jesus. It was He that spoiled the principalities and powers of evil.

"And having spoiled principalities and powers, he made a shew of them openly, triumphing over them in it." **Colossians 2:15**

It was He that died for our sins as a penalty.

"For he hath made him to be sin for us, who knew no sin; that we might be made the righteousness of God in him." **II Cor. 5:21**

It was Jesus that gave His followers authority over unclean spirits and sent them out two by two.

"And he called unto him the twelve, and began to send them forth by two and two; and gave them power over unclean spirits;" **Mark 6:7**

It was Jesus that said,

"And I will pray the Father, and he shall give you another Comforter, that he may abide with you for ever." **John 14:16**

This other comforter is none other than the Holy Spirit that baptized the 120 in the upper room on the day of Pentecost.

Now Hear This…When the Spirit came on the day of Pentecost, He filled everyone with His presence and power. They spoke in other tongues and eventually went out from the upper room to preach, teach, do miracles and walk in the Spirit. Jesus did not abandon them.

He sent His Holy Spirit to deliver His power and authority to His church and to become the source of continued power to live in Christ. You cannot live a victorious Christian Life without this power.

Listen to what Paul said to Timothy.

"For God has not given us a spirit of fear, but of power and of love and of a sound mind. **II Timothy 1:7**

"This is the word of the Lord to Zerubbabel: 'Not by might nor by power, but by My Spirit,' Says the Lord of hosts." **Zechariah 4:6**

Thus, our authority is given by God, through Jesus and made accessible through the Holy Spirit. Jesus has given this authority to us, His followers.

Luke 9:1, 2 says, *"Then he called his twelve disciples together, and gave them power and **authority** over all devils, and to cure* *diseases. And he sent them to preach the kingdom of God, and to heal the sick."*

"And he said unto them, Go ye into all the world, and preach the gospel to every creature. ... *And these signs shall follow them that believe;* In my name shall they cast out devils; they shall speak with new tongues; they shall take up serpents; and if they drink any deadly thing, it shall not hurt them; they shall lay hands on the sick, and they shall recover." **Mark 16:15, 17, 18**.

Clearly, Jesus has promised His authority to those who are His own. The problem is that many Christians do not believe it, and therefore do not exercise it effectively.

They refuse to believe that Christ's authority belongs to the Church today -- although there is no Scripture that in any way hints that His authority would not be available to the Church through all ages.

Many are content to get goose bumps by reading about the miracles that take place in third world countries when the authority of Jesus is put to use.

Some of us may go so far as to dare to command a sickness or a devil to be gone from someone we are praying for, but we are fairly complacent when nothing happens. It is what we were expecting anyway, isn't it? What we are forgetting is that the devil is not a law-abiding citizen. He is, "The Lawless One."

Jesus Himself is the one who has given us authority in His Name. Sometimes -- in fact, most of the time -- there *is* going to be a fight. Hell doesn't want to let go of its victims.

Remember whose authority it is in which we operate. We have no authority to come against the powers of darkness in our own strength. We come against them in the *Name of Jesus*. It is His authority, not ours.

Too often Christians just hang on and try to do the best they can, not realizing their inheritance in Christ. They are to be the head and not the tail. Instead of taking their rightful place in Christ as victors, they magnify the devil, and that gives him access in their lives.

If you dwell on the negative side of things, you will become what you dwell on. What you are thinking about and dwelling on is what you believe. What you believe is what you are talking about and eventually what you believe and talk about is what you become.

This applies in the area of demons and demonic activity too. If you think the devil's thoughts, you will become depressed, oppressed, and you can get into error.

Or you can think on the Word, and your thinking will become enlightened, illuminated, and flooded with light.

You can go around preaching how powerful the devil is, or you can get on the positive side where the eyes of your understanding have been enlightened to see the wisdom of God. Then you will be on the scriptural side and the victory side where you belong as a believer.

Because I know Jesus defeated the devil, that's what I think on and talk about. And the Lord, who is greater, causes me to succeed because I'm giving place to God and the power of His Word, not to the devil.

Exposing The Enemy

Who is the enemy? Ephesians 6:12 says,

"We do not wrestle against flesh and blood, but against principalities, against powers, against the rulers of the darkness of this age, against spiritual hosts of wickedness in the heavenly places."

The devil is the real enemy!

Like A Roaring Lion

1 Peter 5:8-9 (NIV) advises us to: *"Be self-controlled and alert. Your enemy the devil prowls around like a roaring lion looking for someone to devour. Resist him, standing firm in the faith…"*

Notice that this verse does not say the devil is a roaring lion. It says he is like a roaring lion. He wants to make you believe he has more power than he really does, and he manages to fool the majority of people. The truth is, the devil's only weapon is that of deception. He has no legal authority over believers.

When Jesus died and rose again, He not only saved you from an eternity in hell, He also redeemed you from Satan's power and dominion over you on the earth. **1 John 3:8** tells us,

"For this purpose the Son of God was manifested, that He might destroy the works of the devil."

Not only that, but it is recorded in Colossians 2:15 that Jesus "disarmed principalities and powers," and "He made a public spectacle of them, triumphing over them…"

The devil is already defeated, and his power has been dismantled by the finished work of Christ on the cross.

You Have Authority

Jesus said, *"Behold, I give you the authority to trample on serpents and scorpions, and over all the power of the enemy, and nothing shall by any means hurt you"* (Luke 10:19).

That is a great deal of authority!

How is it, then, that the devil is able to keep causing believers so much trouble? It is because many do not exercise the authority God has given them. They are not walking in the understanding that, even though Jesus won the victory, they need to apply that victory in their daily lives.

Think of it this way: it is illegal for someone to break into your house, but don't you still lock your doors to discourage thieves and to protect your property?

In the same way, when it comes to Satan trying to gain entrance into your life, you need to exercise your blood-bought right to close the door in his face. By resisting the devil and standing firm in the faith, you are actively applying or enforcing Jesus' victory.

God has given you all the authority you need to be able to stand against the devil and his works. He has also provided you with armor and spiritual weapons for your warfare against Satan. In his letter to the Ephesians, the apostle Paul describes these items and defines how to use them.

He writes, *"Be strong in the Lord and in the power of His might. Put on the whole armor of God that you may be able to stand against the wiles of the devil. Take up the whole armor of God, that you may be able to withstand in the evil day, and having done all, to stand"* **(Ephesians 6:10-11, 13).**

Paul made it clear that, while God has provided the armor, it is the believer's responsibility to put it on and stand against the enemy. We must take our position of authority and use what God has given us.

In The Name of Jesus

The name of Jesus is powerful. Philippians 2:9-10 says,

"Therefore God also has highly exalted Him and given Him the name which is above every name, that at the name of Jesus every knee should bow, of those in heaven, and of those on earth, and of those under the earth..."

When you use Jesus' name, Satan and all of his demons have to flee.

Kick The Devil Out

Ephesians 4:27 tells us not to give any place to the devil. You do not want to be one who unintentionally gives the devil access by entertaining sin, by being disobedient, or by rebelling against God. Make sure you are quick to forgive others as Christ has forgiven you because having an unwillingness to forgive others can give the devil a foothold in your life **(Mark 11:25)**.

James 4:7 instructs us to, *"Submit to God. Resist the devil and he will flee from you."*

Because Jesus resisted the devil by submitting to God, He could say, *"...he (the devil) has nothing in Me"* **(John 14:30)**.

He left no room for the devil to take advantage of Him. Likewise, when you submit to God and resist the devil in the authority Christ has given you, the devil must leave.

Finally...

The victory Christ won, He won for you. After He rose from the grave, victorious over death, sin, and the grave, He proclaimed,

"All authority has been given to Me in heaven and on earth" **(Matthew 28:18)**.

When you received Christ as the Lord of your life, **Colossians 1:13** says you were delivered from the power of darkness and conveyed into God's kingdom.

You can take a bold stand against the devil and his works because of your position in Christ and because you have been given authority over Satan in the name of Jesus.

As **Proverbs 28:1** says, *"The wicked flee when no one pursues, but the righteous are bold as a lion."*

Submit to God, boldly exercise the authority He has given you, and stand firm because,

"He who is in you is greater than he who is in the world"

(1 John 4:4).

How and When Authority Operates

Today's Christians want instant results. I prayed for healing so why didn't it happen? It's been 10 minutes already with no change. I thought it would be NOW not later or not at all. HOW does this Authority/Power, work? WHEN will I see results?

Sometimes there is a pathway on which we must walk to our healing or to see results. Sometimes we see it immediately. The final result is up to God. We are to pray, believe and proclaim in the name of Jesus. He will make it happen as He sees fit.

I can remember a time we prayed for a lady to be healed. It actually took seven months of continual prayer and continual proclaiming of God's Word. My wife prayed for a lady's leg and vein problems. She was healed in that very hour.

The point is, don't give up because you do not see any change. You declare the Word, Believe the Word and Stand in faith until what you have declared comes into existence. (For we walk by faith, not by sight:) **II Corinthians. 5:7**

Remember, it is the Word that carries all the power and it is your faith and trust in Jesus that what He said is true that gives you the authority.

Bible References Related To The Believer's Authority

Mark 16:17 ...And these signs will accompany those who believe: in my name they will cast out demons; they will speak in new tongues;

James 4:7 ...Submit yourselves therefore to God. Resist the devil, and he will flee from you.

Luke 10:19 ...Behold, I have given you authority to tread on serpents and scorpions, and over all the power of the enemy, and nothing shall hurt you.

Matthew 16:19 ...I will give you the keys of the kingdom of heaven, and whatever you bind on earth shall be bound in heaven, and whatever you loose on earth shall be loosed in heaven."

1 Peter 5:8 ...Be sober-minded; be watchful. Your adversary the devil prowls around like a roaring lion, seeking someone to devour.

Luke 10:19-21 ... "Behold, I have given you authority to tread on serpents and scorpions, and over all the power of the enemy, and nothing shall hurt you. Nevertheless, do not rejoice in this, that the spirits are subject to you, but rejoice that your names are written in heaven." In that same hour he rejoiced in the Holy Spirit and said, "I thank you, Father, Lord of heaven and earth, that you have hidden these things from the wise and understanding and revealed them to little children; yes, Father, for such was your gracious will."

1 John 4:4 ... Little children, you are from God and have overcome them, for he who is in you is greater than he who is in the world.

Revelation 12:11 ...And they have conquered him by the blood of the Lamb and by the word of their testimony, for they loved not their lives even unto death.

Mark 11:23 ...Truly, I say to you, whoever says to this mountain, 'Be taken up and thrown into the sea,' and does not doubt in his heart, but believes that what he says will come to pass, it will be done for him.

Hebrews 4:12 For the word of God is living and active, sharper than any two-edged sword, piercing to the division of soul and of spirit, of joints and of marrow, and discerning the thoughts and intentions of the heart.

Acts 1:8 ... "But you will receive power when the Holy Spirit has come upon you, and you will be my witnesses in Jerusalem and in all Judea and Samaria, and to the end of the earth."

John 14:12 ..."Truly, truly, I say to you, whoever believes in me will also do the works that I do; and greater works than these will he do, because I am going to the Father."

Mark 6:13 ...And they cast out many demons and anointed with oil many who were sick and healed them.

Ephesians 6:10-18 ...Finally, be strong in the Lord and in the strength of his might. Put on the whole armor of God, that you may be able to stand against the schemes of the devil. For we do not wrestle against flesh and blood, but against the rulers, against the authorities, against the cosmic powers over this present darkness, against the spiritual forces of evil in the heavenly places.

Therefore take up the whole armor of God, that you may be able to withstand in the evil day, and having done all, to stand firm. Stand therefore, having fastened on the belt of truth, and having put on the breastplate of righteousness, ...

Matthew 28:18-20 ...And Jesus came and said to them, "All authority in heaven and on earth has been given to me. Go therefore and make disciples of all nations, baptizing them in the name of the Father and of the Son and of the Holy Spirit, teaching them to observe all that I have commanded you. And behold, I am with you always, to the end of the age."

Psalm 91:13 ...You will tread on the lion and the adder; the young lion and the serpent you will trample underfoot.

OUR GREATEST FAN

God is faithful
Even when we are not.
He watches over His Word,
Crossing every "T" and every "Dot."

He is a very present help
In times of sorrow and pain.
We can trust in His Word
For sunshine and latter rain.

He alone holds our future
In the palms of His hands.
He leads us as a loving Shepherd
Into green pastures and fruitful lands

God is faithful
To honor His covenant with man.
He, though LORD of all,
Is our greatest fan.

Written By
John Marinelli

CHAPTER FOUR

Resting In The Lord

Living a victorious Christian life is all about resting in the Lord. There is a rest that God has provided for His children. However, this rest is only for those who walk with the Lord by faith. If you are a sometimes Christian with very little biblical knowledge, you will most likely miss out on God rest.

You cannot stumble into the rest of God. The Lord has to lead you there. That means you have to be tuned into hearing His voice and willing to obey His commands. Otherwise, you will stray off in another direction by yourself. Now let's look at the scriptural support for such a notion.

> *"The Lord is my shepherd; I shall not want. He makes me to lie down in green pastures: he leads me beside the still waters. He restores my soul: he leads me in the paths of righteousness for his name's sake. Yea, though I walk through the valley of the shadow of death, I will fear no evil: for thou art with me; thy rod and thy staff they comfort me. Thou prepare a table before me in the presence of mine enemies: thou anoint my head with oil; my cup runs over. Surely goodness and mercy shall follow*

me all the days of my life: and I will dwell in the house of the Lord forever." **Psalm 23**

Psalm 23 is probably the most well known text in the Holy Scriptures. This is a most beloved psalm and has been quoted in almost every conceivable venue where people need hope. Many a soldier has carried it into battle or placed it next to his heart in a foxhole. Hospitals and funeral homes are also often places of recital.

There was a time when every school child would learn it and say it as a daily routine. Sadly, those days are mostly gone because of our government's hatred of all things Godly. However, disdain for the Bible does not diminish the spiritual impact made by its words.

Some folks fear turning their lives over to God because He might lead them somewhere they do not want to go. The 23rd psalm tells us that being led by God is a rewarding experience. We end up in green pastures (Prosperity) and lie down by still waters (Peace-no confusion); Our souls (Mind, Will & Emotions) are restored;

The fear of evil fades away; Goodness and mercy follow us through life; we even have a feast while our enemies look on and finally we dwell with the Lord forever. That's a pretty good deal, don't you think?

God's Rest Is Not For Everyone

God does not lead the masses into His rest. He leads His Children. He must be your shepherd. That makes you His sheep. Being a sheep has certain indicators that prove you are really a sheep and not a wolf:

1. Sheep hear their Shepherd's voice.

2. Sheep come to their Shepherd's call.

3. Sheep do not question their Shepherd's commands.

4. Sheep know when the wolf is near and cries for the Shepherd.

The atheist, agnostic, pantheist and all others that reject Jesus Christ as well as disobedient Christians do not and will not follow His lead. Thus, they miss out on the rest of God.

The rest of God spoken of in scriptures is a blessing of fellowship and a benefit to only those that are fully persuaded that He (God) is able and willing to protect and guide them through life.

God's Promise of Rest

Hebrews 4:1-11

"Therefore, since a promise remains of entering His rest, let us fear lest any of you seem to have come short of it. For indeed the gospel was preached to us as well as to them; but the word, which they heard did not profit them, not being mixed with faith in those who heard it.

For we who have believed do enter that rest, as He has said: although the works were finished from the foundation of the world. So I swore in My wrath, They shall not enter My rest, For He has spoken in a certain place of the seventh day in this way: "And God rested on the seventh day from all His works"; and again in this place: "They shall not enter My rest".

Since therefore it remains that some must enter it, and those to whom it was first preached did not enter because of unbelief, again He designates a certain day, saying in David, "Today," after such a long time, as it has been said: Today, if you will hear His voice, do not harden your hearts.

For if Joshua had given them rest, then He would not afterward have spoken of another day. There remains therefore a rest for the people of God. For he who has entered His rest has himself also ceased from his works as God did from His.

Let us therefore be diligent to enter that rest, lest anyone fall according to the same example of disobedience.

We are encouraged to rest from all our works because God rested from all His works. The promise from God is that we can really enter into His rest and because He did, we can too.

However, sometimes we have to labor to enter in. Why? Because we get so caught up in what we are doing that it becomes really hard to just sit back and leave it up to God.

Someone may be wondering what, " all our works" is. It is not getting up and going to work every day or being a reliable husband or wife.

The rest is from trying to attain salvation by our own efforts. God took care of that in His master plan before the foundation of the world. His redemptive plan for man was to sacrifice His only Son as a penalty for sin and offer His salvation to all who would believe. **(John 3:16)**

To rest then is to believe that Jesus was sacrificed for our sin and accept Him as our savior. We are to put our trust in Him and stop trying to buy God's favor with good works. **(Ephesians 2:8-9)**

That which we are to let go of is the anxiety, fear, confusion, worry and control over our own lives. We are to step off the throne of our life. That seat is now reserved for Jesus. We can trust Him because He said from the cross; **"It Is Finished"** which fulfilled God's rest from all His works on the 7th day of creation. He already made plans for us to rest in Him.

"God made him who had no sin to be sin for us, so that in him we might become the righteousness of God" **(2 Corinthians 5:21)**.

We can now cease from our spiritual labors and rest in Him, not just one day a week, but every day.

Spiritually Speaking

Let's look at the spiritual applications of resting in the Lord. As Christians, we have made Jesus Lord and seek to walk with Him through this life. However, evil is on every side and it is hard to live out our faith in Christ.

We strive to make ends meet. We worry over our children and their future. We hope that sickness or sorrow will not knock on our door. We are anxious, fearful, and when someone says to us, "How are you doing today?" we reply with, "I am just hanging in there."

This is a word picture of a Christian without faith. They are doing just what the Old Testament saints did, not believing. Their unbelief kept them from entering into God's rest. We can fall into the same scenario and miss out on the promise.

How We Enter In

Our labor to enter in is believing. What do we believe? We believe that God rested on the 7th day from all His work. That means His master plan was complete. It means that God saw every need, every situation and every prayer in His foreknowledge and scheduled them for action in His master plan.

The Law was seen long before it appeared. In the fullness of time, it came to expose sin and bring death to all that sin. **(Lev.18:20)**

Accordingly, in the fullness of time, Christ came with a new law…the law of the Spirit of Life that brought us liberty and salvation. **(Romans 8:2)**

This new law set us free from the old one. However, both were in God's master plan waiting to be released.

Thus it is with our daily lives. We are in God's master plan and He works everything together for our good and His glory. **(Romans 8:28)** All we have to do is trust in Jesus; believe that He is in control; and wait for the manifestation of our deliverance.

We enter in by faith and we remain at rest by faith knowing that the battle is the Lords and He is our shield.

Jesus is our shield against evil and lack in this life. He will provide. He will lead us to green pastures and still waters. He will restore our souls.

Unbelieving Christians

The Bible tells us that some of the Old Testament saints did not believe and they perished in the wilderness. They never entered the rest of God that was promised to them. They never entered the "Promised Land."

However, the amazing thing was that God still took care of them in the wilderness. Their shoes did not wear out. Nor did their clothing. They ate manna from heaven. Not one was feeble in mind or spirit. They still died in the wilderness. Here's what this says to me:

Life can be good but you can still die in the wilderness

It is better to fear (reverence) God than to fear giants and men of power and authority that dwell in your future.

God's blessings are always connected with faith. No faith, no promise, no divine destiny.

Fear will hinder faith. They are two sides to the same coin. But faith crushes fear and brings victory.

One's destiny lies in his or her own hands. We choose the path to walk in life and what lies at the end of the road. Life or death is in the power of our own choices.

God is looking for partners to rule the earth and has chosen us, His children…those who are willing to stand with Him.

REST MY CHILD

Rest my child, says the Lord.
Take thy peace and be restored.
I have provided, thy mouth to feed.
From the beginning, I knew your need.

Do not worry, fret or even fear,
For, my child, I am always near,
To bless thy soul with love and grace,
To be with thee, face to face.

Come, my child, near to my throne.
Do not allow your faith to roam.
For those who will not believe
Can never find rest in times of need.

My Word shall see you through.
My grace I freely give to you,
That you should rest, thy soul to keep,
Forever delivered from unbelief.

Written By
John Marinelli

Benefits of Entering Into God's Rest

1. We have continual access into God's rest where we find peace.

2. We gain a new perspective on life and eternity.

3. We do not beat ourselves up when we fall short.

4. We start being who we are in Christ and not what others think we are.

5. We have true fellowship with God and we rest in His grace.

6. We see God at work fighting our battles for us. The battle is the Lords.

As we rest in God, we grow in grace. We see His hand in our lives and hear His voice. All of this makes us more thankful than ever before.

Our praise and adoration for God is because we know that *"If it had not been the Lord"*, we would not have been able to stand.

I am sure you can find more benefits. Mine are just some that I know to be true.

It was Jesus that completed the Law and opened up the door of grace for those who believed in Him. He was the one that lived the life that God expected man to live, a righteous life.

He was the only one that could die for the sins of mankind, because He was, as it were, the spotless Lamb of God, that was foreshadowed in the Hebrew sacrifices of the Old Testament. It was He that became the Captain of our Salvation and Lord of Heaven and Earth.

The only thing we are instructed to fear is unbelief. We always want to believe regardless of what we see or feel. God is always with us and He alone is in control. This is the perspective that should rule our lives and shape our actions. Unbelief has no place in our Spiritual walk with Jesus. We walk by faith and not by sight. **II Corinthians 5:7**

CHAPTER FIVE

Hearing The Voice of God

Is God speaking to people today? Is anybody listening? If God were speaking to you, what do you think He'd be saying? Is it too way out to say, *"I am hearing from God"?* After all, He is the creator of all things. He is the "Supreme Ruler" of the universe. Why would He want to talk to you? How do you know, for sure, that the voice in your head is the voice of God?

We are left here on planet earth, seemingly, all alone to fend for ourselves. It's a make it or break it existence with a future in serious doubt.

Is that how you feel? I used to think and feel like that...like... Why do I exist? Why am I here in this place and at this time? Do I have a purpose in life? Or am I just drifting with the masses towards an unknown destiny?

Well... I do not think or feel that way anymore. I was a teenager back then with very little knowledge or wisdom. It's been over 60 years since I felt lost and alone and without hope.

Things changed when I accepted Jesus as my Lord and Savior. He led me to the Bible and I, not only discovered my existence and purpose, but also my destiny. I realized that I didn't have to walk alone through a world that is less than perfect. ***I found myself in God.***

As I search, prayed and sought after truth, I began to hear from God. He started speaking directly to my spirit in ways I never knew were even possible. This divine fellowship, between God and me, proved to me that it was all very real and that I was really a "Child of God."

The Witness of The Spirit

Romans 8:16, helped me a lot because it said that God would show Himself to me so I would know that I know that I am in His loving care.

"The Spirit itself bears witness with our spirit, that we are children of God." Romans 8:16

Here it is in the World English Bible…*"The Spirit himself testifies with our spirit that we are children of God;"*

I am sure you are wondering how the Spirit of God testifies or bears witness. It's kind of hard to explain. I guess the most significant would be answered prayer. When you are praying about a thing, asking for a specific result, and He brings it into reality, you can't help but acknowledge that it was His doing.

I have seen the hand of the Lord in my life, moving on my behalf, to deliver me from harm and bless me in ways that were so clearly His work of grace.

Then there's the Bible. You haven't lived until you read the scriptures and certain promises seem to leap off the page into your heart. You just know that the Holy Spirit is speaking to you and often it is concerning a specific problem or request. God's counsel and guidance becomes alive as you read.

Channels of Communication

God speaks to us in many different ways. If we are aware of them, we will be more apt to listen. Here are the three most important ways to consider:

The Bible ...First and foremost is the Holy Scriptures. This is where you discover God. His story, actions, character, and love are all clearly revealed. It is a great source of counsel and wisdom.

Divine Unction ... The Holy Spirit will drop a thought or even an answer to a situation directly into your heart. You will have a peace about it and you will just know that you know it is from God. This is, for sure, a non-verbal communication.

God's Messenger ... God will often send a messenger with a "Word" of truth. The messenger could be the pastor of a church in a sermon, a Bible Study Teacher, a Godly friend, an angel in a dream, a vision, and so on. However, be sure that the message lines up with the knowledge of God. It cannot contradict the truths set forth in the Bible. If it does, it is not from God.

If we desire to hear the voice of God, we must open our hearts. We do not hear with our ears. It is the heart that listens. As "Children of God", our hearts cry out for the living God. He is our Father and friend. It is His hand that guides us, helps us, and delivers us. He is the source of our blessings and very existence.

Many folks do not hear from God because they do not want to know. God, for them, is at arm's length and sought after only in a crisis. Day-to-day involvement with God is not on their agenda. Jesus as Lord is, to them, a slogan, not a lifestyle. This has been true for centuries. Here's what Jesus said back when He was on the earth.

"He that hath ears to hear. Let him hear." Matthew 11:15

He said this because they were not listening. They didn't have their ears attached to their hearts.

You have to have ears in order to hear but your ears need to be attached to your heart…meaning, this is a serious matter and it needs your full attention.

There are a few things you can do to make it easier to hear the voice of God. Consider these:

Establish a Quiet Time…In today's self-driven world where everything is fast paced and rushed; it can be hard to hear from God. Although, your ultimate goal is to hear His voice in any circumstance. However, you have to start somewhere and a quiet time is a good place to meditate on the Word and listen.

Stop The Mental Traffic Flow… The devil tries to keep our minds flowing with needless noise. As long as we are thinking about lots of meaningless things, we will not have the time to listen for the, "Still Small Voice" of God. Stop the mind chatter and listen.

Focus on God…Seek Him while He may be found. Don't wait for Him to come to you. Engage in prayer and ask Him to share Himself with you. This will shut out everything else and clear the channel between you and God. This action is Biblical.

Hear the words of Jesus...

"Ask, and it shall be given you; seek, and ye shall find; knock, and it shall be opened unto you: For every one that asks receives; and he that seeks finds; and to him that knocks, it shall be opened." Matthew 7:7-8

Accept God's Will... If we do not want to accept God's will, He most likely will not tell us His will. It is clearly revealed in the Bible. However, He wants to share that with you personally from His heart.

Hearing God's voice
What To Do Next

Call Upon The Holy Spirit... We were given the Holy Spirit at our New Birth (When we accepted Jesus) It's ok to call upon the Holy Spirit to interpret our prayers, heal our wounds, and help us to hear from God. He was given to us for that purpose.

Learn To Recognize God's Voice... You can recognize His voice among all the other voices coming and going through your mind. It just takes practice. Here's what John, the apostle said...

"Beloved, believe not every spirit, (Thought/voices) but try the spirits, (Thoughts/voices) whether they are of God: because many false prophets are gone out into the world." I John 4:1

God wants you to examine every thought and every voice because all thoughts are not yours. They also enter your mind from Satan, The Flesh, Other's Expectations and of course, God. The one to act upon is the one that brings you the most peace. If you feel fear, anxiety, confusion or guilt, reject it and cast it out immediately. Do not entertain it.

Be Filled With The Spirit... God wants us to be continually filled with His Holy Spirit. This is a daily if not moment-by-moment process. We need to walk in His Spirit, Live in His Spirit, and apply all that He reveals to us. Listen to what Paul said to the Ephesians. There's a new song in your future.

"And be not drunk with wine, wherein is excess; but be filled with the Spirit; Speaking to yourselves in psalms and hymns and spiritual songs, singing and making melody in your heart to the Lord; Giving thanks always for all things unto God and the Father in the name of our Lord Jesus Christ;" Ephesians 5:18-20

Being filled is a "Be, Being" action verb... meaning allow God to continually fill you. In other words, one time is not enough. It has to be a steady flow of Holy Ghost power to keep you filled and ready to face the world.

When You Don't Hear His Voice

What happens when you just cannot discern which voice in your head is God's? Sometimes, God wants us to use our minds to search for an answer. He will give us indicators and expect us to draw our own conclusion based upon the knowledge of God already revealed. Here are a few indicators that will help you to know if the voice you are hearing is from God:

1. Is what's being said contrary to Biblical truth? If so, it is not God talking to you.

2. Is what's being said causing confusion, doubt or anxiety? If so, it's not from God. God's voice always brings peace and has a tone of love and care.

3. Is what's being said putting you under false expectations or is oppressing you in any way? If so, it's not from God.

Do you feel good about doing what is being said? If you are afraid and feel a sense of guilt if you participate in whatever is being asked of you, it's not of God.

Remember, the devil will always lie to you and suggest that you participate in some sort of immorality. It could be anything from telling a lie to stealing to even sex or murder. His goal is to tear down what God has built up in you.

God's voice, on the other hand, always encourages, builds up, strengthens, and is always in an attitude of peace.

Missing Out Is Not An Option

You should never feel sad about missing the Voice of God. Here what the scriptures say:

"So shall my word be that goes forth out of my mouth: it shall not return unto me void, but it shall accomplish that which I please, and it shall prosper in the thing whereto I sent it." **Isaiah 55:11**

God knows who you are, where you are and what you are doing. If He wants to talk to you, you will not miss His Word because He says it will not come back to Him void but will accomplish that to which He sends it.

Jesus put it this way, *"My sheep hear my voice, and I know them, and they follow Me."* John 10:27

If you are His, you will hear Him when He calls. Why? Because the shepherd trains the sheep to listen for His voice among many other voices. That is what the Holy Spirit does when He bears witness with our spirit. He is teaching us to discern the voice of God.

"The steps of a good man are ordered by the Lord, And He

delights in his way. Though he fall, he shall not be utterly cast down; For the Lord upholds him with His hand" Psalm 37:23-24

God will order our steps, and even when we blow it, if we are truly trying to do His will, He will lift us up and give us a second chance.

Knowing Comes From Commitment

"Commit thy works unto the LORD, and thy thoughts shall be established." Proverbs 16:3

If our thoughts are established, we will know that we know what the will of the Lord is and we will already be in close communication with God, our Father who loves us. Paul tells us in Romans how to commit...

"I beseech (Beg) you therefore, brethren, by the mercies of God, that ye present your bodies a living sacrifice, holy, acceptable unto God, which is your reasonable service. And be not conformed to this world: but be ye transformed by the renewing of your mind, that ye may prove what is that good, and acceptable, and perfect, will of God." **Romans 12:1-2**

It is so much easier to hear when we are submitted to God and His will for our lives. I can remember a story from the Old Testament about a disobedient prophet. God finally opened the mouth of an Ass and rebuked him. (Numbers 22:28-30) We don't want God to have to speak through an Ass before we will listen. It is better to hear and obey and keep the favor of God upon us.

The God Who Speaks

God is speaking, whereas Idols do not speak because God is alive and Idols are not. God Himself is known as "The Word", and His speech commanded nothing to produce everything (John 1:1–3).

"The voice of the Lord is powerful; the voice of the Lord is full of majesty" (Psalm 29:4). When God wants the dead to come to life he says, "Live!" (Ezekiel 16:6), and when Jesus wanted his friend to walk out of the grave, he spoke, "Lazarus, come out" (John 11:43). Even now, Jesus is holding together your molecules with his words (Hebrews 1:3). If Jesus were to stop speaking, you would stop existing.

A Still Small Voice

There is only one place in Scripture where God is said to have spoken in a *"Still Small Voice,"* It was to Elijah after his dramatic victory over the prophets of Baal (1 Kings 18:20-40);

God is not confined to a single manner of communicating. Elsewhere in Scripture, He is said to communicate through a whirlwind (Job 38:1), to announce His presence by an earthquake (Exodus 19:18), and to speak in a voice that sounds like thunder (1 Samuel 2:10; Job 37:2; Psalm 104:7; John 12:29). In Psalm 77:18 His voice is compared to both thunder and a whirlwind and in Revelation 4:5, we're told that lightning and thunder proceed from the throne in heaven.

Nor is God limited to natural phenomena when He speaks. All through the Old Testament, He speaks through His prophets. The common thread in all the prophets is the phrase, *"Thus says the Lord."* He speaks through the writers of Scripture. Most graciously, however, He speaks through His Son, the Lord Jesus. The writer to the Hebrews opens his letter with this truth:

"Long ago, at many times and in many ways, God spoke to our

fathers by the prophets, but in these last days he has spoken to us by his Son, whom he appointed the heir of all things, through whom also he created the world" (Hebrews 1:1–2).

Hebrews 1:1-2 tells us that the voice we are hearing is the voice of Jesus. Hebrews says this…

"Keep your lives free from the love of money and be content with what you have, because God has said, "Never will I leave you; never will I forsake you. So we say with confidence, "The Lord is my helper; I will not be afraid. What can mere mortals do to me?" Hebrews 13:5-6 NIV

It is less important to know how God speaks to us than it is to know what we should do with what He says. God speaks most clearly to us in our day through His Word, the Bible. The more we learn it, the more ready we will be to recognize His voice when He speaks, and the more likely we are to obey what we hear.

Don't wait for something to happen. **"Ask, Knock & Seek"** the Lord until heaven opens and you hear His voice. This is His Will that you do so.

> *"What shall we then say to these things?*
> *If God be for us, who can be against us?"*
> **Romans 8:31**

Hello my child,
How are you today?
I waited for your call
And have much to say.

A word in due season,
To cause your faith to soar.
A morsel of truth,
To quiet the lion's roar.

So hear, my beloved,
Before you go on life's way,
For there's a special blessing
In what I have to say.

It's not by might nor by power,
That you should gain success.
But it's by my Holy Spirit
That you attain life's very best.

Ask me now, my child,
For all that you need,
For I bless everyone
Who is willing to believe.

Written By
John Marinelli

CHAPTER SIX

Being, "Born Again"

There is a great falling away from the faith in America. Many denominations do not even agree on Jesus being the only way to God. The gospel has been diluted into a "Social Gospel" that promotes the notion that every person is a child of God no matter what religion or denomination.

You Must Be "Born Again"

> *"Jesus answered and said unto him, Verily, verily, I say unto thee, except a man be born again, he cannot see the kingdom of God".* **John 3:3**

This false doctrine that everyone is a child of God drives our political, racial, and economic worlds so as to destroy the very fabric of true faith and Biblical truth. Instead of God being supreme, man has opted to become his own god.

This theological premise is not limited to the non-Christian world. It has also invaded the church. If you are surprised to learn these facts, let me share a few statistics from the PEW report, a well known organization that tracts trends and movement in religion.

The PEW Research Report

This report says that 78% of all Catholics do not identify themselves as being, "Born Again". Nor do 51% of all Methodists, 55% of all Presbyterians, 63% of all Lutherans, 29% of all Adventists and 29% of all Restorationists see themselves as "Born Again". These folks will not see the kingdom of God because they are not, "Born Again" by their own admission.

So What Does It Mean To Be, "Born Again"?

To be "Born Again" is to undergo a "spiritual birth", or a <u>regeneration</u> of the human spirit by the power of the <u>Holy Spirit</u>. This is contrasted with the physical birth everyone experiences. It referrs to being converted to a personal faith in Christ which causes the new birth to occur. It requires repentence from personal sin and accepting Jesus as Lord and Savor.

This report shows clearly that many of those who claim Christianity have fallen away from its roots and slipped off its foundation which is Christ. They still dwell in darkness and live in the flesh supporting a religious but carnal lifestyle.

I suggest you read my eBooks on How To Be Born Again, Left Behind, and The Incarnation of Christ to gain a more complete perspective. You can download them free at:

<u>www.christianliferesourcecenter.org.</u>

The point is, they have fallen away or never knew true faith, much less the importance of practicing the Lordship of Christ.

Why Should We Make Jesus Lord Over Our Life?

When we truly are "Born Again" we want to please God. Our

entire experience is based upon repentence. We openly admit to God that we have fallen short of His righteousness and are sorry for all the sin and rebellion we have participated in. Some of us would admit that we did a very bad job of managing our own lives.

We didn't have the forsight to make good decisions. We got caught up into demonic snares like drugs, alcohol, imoral sex, hate, and all the other evils of this world. In short, we made a mess of things and now are in need of a Savior that will come and take charge and straighten things out.

Benefits of Jesus As Our Lord And Savor

No Worrying...You don't have to worry about everything that comes up. Our trust is in Jesus. He will handle it.

Divine Power ... to overcome bad habits and temtations.

Peace of Mind... because you now can rest, knowing that all things will work together for your good. (Romans 8:28)

Ringside Seat... in the battle of the ages as the Lord Himself fights your battle with evil forces. (Psalm 27:1-3)

Enhansed Relationship... with Christ because you are walking closer to Him and listening for His voice.

Personal Satisfaction... knowing that you are pleasing the Lord and honoring Him.

Special Revelation... as the Holy Spirit gives you words to say and a course of actions to take in troubling situations.

Answered Prayer...Being in tune with the Holy Spirit brings answers to our prayers in a clear and understandible way.

The idea of the Lordship of Christ… it does not consist of one act of obedience but rather is measured by the sum of our obedience, and it cannot be accomplished in our own strength or power, but by the power available to us by the indwelling Holy Spirit. We are strongest when we are relying on Him (2 Corinthians 12:10).

All or Nothing

Being a Christian is no joke. It is not a, "get out of jail" card in some quasi monopoly game of life. It is an all or nothing situation.

You cannot live life with one foot in a world of carnality and the other in the spiritual realm. Jesus said,

"He that is not with me is against me; and he that gathers not with me scatters abroad. Matthew 12:30

There is no in-between. No neutral ground. We are with Him or against Him.

There are lots of folks that play church, talking the talk, acting as though they understand but fail in the final analysis. It's like what Jesus said to the scribes and Pharisees of His day,

"Woe to you, scribes and Pharisees, hypocrites! For you clean the outside of the cup and of the dish, but inside they are full of robbery and self-indulgence." NASV Matthew 20:25

We do not want to be like them. Christianity is an absolute surrender to God. Jesus said,

"For whosoever will save his life shall lose it: and whosoever will lose his life for my sake shall find it." Matthew 16:25

He also said, *"If any man will come after me, let him deny himself, and take up his cross, and follow me."* Matthew 16:24

It is high time that we, you and me and all the other believers, sell out to Jesus and surrender to His will. He will not let us down. He is a loving God, compassionate, caring and gentle in all His ways. His Lordship is in our best interest.

I SURRENDER ALL

I surrender all, oh Lord, to Thee,
My love, my life and my liberty.
For if I should rule life's throne,
I would stand all alone.

But with my will I offer Thee,
My love, my life and destiny.
That you should rule upon my throne.
With love and grace and dignity.

I'd surrender all I have, oh Lord, to Thee,
For but a glimpse of your majesty.
That I may live within your perfect love,
For that's the way it's meant to be.

Yes, I surrender all to Jesus
That he may deliver me
From the curse of sin and death,
That I may live for eternity.

Written By
John Marinelli

CHAPTER SEVEN

Day-By-Day Living

How do I live out my salvation? I try to do good and be good but I can't seem to live the abundant life that Jesus spoke of... Nor do I attain victory in my walk with God. *Why is that?* I go to church, give offerings and even volunteer at times.

If this is you, you are suffering from a lack of knowledge or a faulty mindset that has distorted your thinking. There is always a reason why you fail and why you live a defeated Christian life. Your mindset i.e. <u>the way you think</u> is usually what keeps you from having victory.

This chapter is designed to focus your attention on basic Bible truths that will transform your thinking and set you on a course toward abundant living. You only have to receive these foundational principles and apply them in your daily thought life. This is how you live a victorious Christian Life.

Basic Bible Truths

If you've been a Christian for any length of time, you will have realized that there are basic Bible truths that create a foundation for living life as a follower of Christ.

A basic truth is a fundamental principle that becomes a perspective or mindset. It forms a foundation upon which all other aspects of life rest. Without it, there is no way to live a successful Christian life. We have no place to demonstrate our faith. Let me explain…

A Bible truth is a hook to hang your faith on. It is a word from the Lord meant to establish and keep us on the path to glory. Romans 8:28 is a good example.

"And we know that in all things God works for the good for those who love him, who have been called according to his purpose"

As a Christian, you have been called out from the pagan world to accomplish God's purposes. As a Christian, you are suspose to love God because He first loved you. This qualifies you to receive the promise of the verse…that God will work everything together for good. This is a basic Bible truth that forms a foundation for life that we can believe in. It becomes a mindset and foundation for all of life's experiences.

Other basic Bible truths inclide: The Virgin Birth, The Blood of Christ as a penalty for our sin, That Jesus was pre-existant in heaven as God but became man to save us, that Jesus was crucified on a Roman cross, died and rose again the third day and afterwards assended into heaven, that Jesus will return again to extinguish evil on the earth and set up His kingdom.

There are more, but now I want to focus on specific foundational principles that will set you free if you are in any type of bondage, being physical, emotional or spiritual.

Foundational Principles For Daily By Day Living

Christianity is not a religion. It is a *Walk With God*. It does not boil down to a set of rules and regulations that if broken cause punisment. It is a relationship between you and God.

Jesus said, *"My sheep hear my voice, and I know them, and they follow me: And I give unto them eternal life; and they shall never perish, neither shall any man pluck them out of my hand."* John 10:27-28

Principle #1… I Am Loved And Accepted By God

Many churchgoers do not know in whom they have believed. Some even think that God is a mean old man, ready to strike out at any infraction, even if it is a small one. However, the Bible says that God is Love and Love is even listed as one of the fruits of His Spirit.

Set your mind to know that God is not mad at you. Tell yourself that He loves you and has your best interest at heart. This is a foundational principle that will bring you much joy and peace, knowing you are loved and accepted by your creator. See John 3:16 It doesn't matter what others think about you. All that matters is what God thinks about you…and He loves you.

Principle #2… The Devil Is An Evil Lying Spirit

Jesus said that He came to earth so we might have life and that life would be abundant. However, He also contrasts His mission with that of the thief/devil. He says, The thief comes but to steel, kill and destroy. John 10:10. So we know that we are marked by the devil for burglary, death and destruction. Ignoring this is not smart. We need to know the tricks of our enemy and how to defeat him. Read my other eBook on The Authority of The Believer. It is on my website, previously given.

Principle #3...I Have Authority Over Evil Spirits

Peter tells us in I Peter 5:8-9 "Be sober, be vigilant; because your adversary the devil, as a roaring lion, walks about, seeking whom he may devour: Whom resist stedfast in the faith, knowing that the same afflictions are accomplished in your brethren that are in the world.

This tells me that the devil is defeated. He may roar like a lion and scare me at times but all I have to do is resist him in the faith and he will run away with his tail betweens his legs. If I understand this, I will have a mindset that grounds me in times of trouble. I can resist by quoting scriptures like Jesus did when He was tempted. I can stand on the known promises of God found in the Bible. Do this and you will have victory.

Principle #4...I Will Let The Peace of God Be The Referee

There are many situations in life that require our attention and decisions. We are always making choices. Do I do this or that? Which is right? Should I take this job or that one? Life's decisions go on and on. However, now we can find God's will in the matters at hand by applying one simple truth. Here's what the scripture says...

"And let the peace of God rule in your hearts, to the which also ye are called in one body; and be ye thankful." Colossians 3:15 One version actually says umpire or referee.

If the peace of God is allowed to referee, it will blow its whistle when you are off sides and call you back. You will know that you are making the wrong decision because you just do not have peace about it.

This mindset is a great weapon against temptation and intimidation from others. If you cannot find peace, drop it, no matter how important it seems at the time. It is not of God and He is telling you to stay away from it.

Principle #5… Confusion Is Not of God

"For God is not the author of confusion, but of peace, as in all churches of the saints." I Corinthians 14:33

Knowing this truth is essential to finding God's will and making good decisions. If you are confused, it is not of God. He does not author or cause confusion. He does author peace and seeks to help you to walk in it at all times. If you suffer under confusion, toss whatever you are confused about out and seek the Lord for His peace.

Principle #6… Fear Is Not from My Heavenly Father.

"For *God* hath *not* given us the spirit of *fear*; but of power, and of love, and of a sound mind." II Timothy 1:7 Ask yourself this question… "If fear is not from God, who does it belong to?" Fear brings torment and the only spirit that uses it is evil. Thus it should be crushed before it takes hold. You can do that by seeking the Lord for a sound mind.

Principle #7…All Things Will Work Together For My Good.

"And we know that in all things God works for the good of those who love him, who have been called according to his purpose" Romans 8:28

God does not cause bad things to happen to us but He will cause them to work together for our benefit. If we have this mindset, we can go on, even in the midst of trouble, knowing that God is with us and is activly working behind it all so we are ultimately be blessed.

I remember a man that was devestated because his marriage ended after many years. He was bitter and blamed God. Many years later, I ran into him and his new wife. He was so happy and said to me, "I couldn't see any good coming from my divorce back then when it happened but now I can see how He worked it all out for my benefit."

Principle # 8... There Must Be A Reason For That.

Have you ever wondered why things happen? Things like someone pulling out onto the highway right in front of you and then slowing down...or like you can't get your car started and are late for work...or having a meeting downtown and it is suddenly cancelled. Do things happen for a reason or are they just happenstance? Here's a real live example from the Bible. It's found in **John 9:1-23**

"Now as *Jesus* passed by, He saw a man who was blind from birth. And His disciples asked Him, saying, "Rabbi, who sinned, this man or his parents, that he was born blind?"

Jesus answered, "Neither this man nor his parents sinned, but that the works of God should be revealed in him. I must work the works of Him who sent me while it is day; *the* night is coming when no one can work. As long as I am in the world, I am the light of the world."

Did you get the picture? Jesus was walking by with His disciples and saw a blind man. His disciples wanted to know why this guy was blind from his birth. Jesus said it was because the works of God should be revealed in him. He was also careful to explain that it was not the guys' fault or his parents.

There is always a reason for what happens to us. The sovereignty of God was at play as God intervened in the blind man's life. You can bet your bottom dollar that when God steps in, He has a good reason for doing so.

Having this mindset kept you at peace because when frustration enters our day and we get irritated, we can return to our rest knowing that There Must Be A Reason For That. It calls us to a posture of submission and invokes an attitude of patience as we wait upon the Lord.

Principle #9... Jesus Is Coming Soon

Jesus told His disciples that He would be crucified, buried and would rise from the dead. He also said that He would go to the Father and prepare a place for us. Finally, He told us that He would return to gather His followers unto Himself.

Christians have been waiting ever since for His return. When that time comes, according to His own testimony, He will separate the sheep from the goats. Then He will invite His sheep to enter into His kingdom that was prepared for them before the foundation of the world. The goats, on the other hand, are to be banished from His sight into an everlasting hell fire.

The reason I added this to my list of foundational principles is because it could be in our lifetime. All the signs point to the fact that He is coming soon.

That one thought can be the inspiration to live a righteous life, in submission to His will, and to comfort ourselves, knowing that He will make all things right. That is to say, those that have hurt us will be punished. We will see their destruction. Good will always win, even if it is at the end of all things.

Principle #10… God's Angels Watch Over Us

Do you believe in angels? I know some folks that say they believe in angels but do not believe in God. Go figure! If angels exist, there has to be a God and if there is a God, there has to be a heaven where He dwells and life eternal because angels are eternal beings.

There is no convincing evidence in Scripture that every person has their own specific guardian angel. There are angels who protect, guard and minister to God's people (Ps. 91:11-12), but the wicked have no angels of God to protect and guide them. They have only demonic spirits that seek to torment them, kill their dreams, steal their peace and destroy their destiny.

Psalm 34:7 tells us that, "The angel of the Lord encamps round about them that fear him, and delivers them." The word, "fear" is also translated, "Reverence". If we reverence or worship God, He will send His own angel to set up a fully operational camp of warring angels. Their sole mission is to protect and deliver you.

Having this mindset is to rest in an upside down world of hate, evil and other ungodly activity. We can thus relax, even in the midst of turmoil.

These ten "Fundamental Principles" make up one powerful mindset. They are the foundation upon which you build your faith and walk with God.

If you apply them they will keep you in His will. They will keep you out of the snares of the devil, and they will help you to experience the joy of the Lord as never before.

If you ignore these "Foundational Principles", you will continue to stumble through life and be tossed to and fro by the turbulence of an ever-raging emotional sea that is full of confusion, fear, and a lot more evil..

God loves us and wants us to walk with Him but He does not take prisoners. We must come to Him freely and completely. Are you ready?

Here's what you need to tell yourself: Let it be your confession of faith, first to yourself and then to the world around you.

Your Confession of Faith

Principle #1... <u>I Am Loved And Accepted By God</u>. What Other Folks Think Just Doesn't Matter.

Principle #2... <u>The Devil Is An Evil Spirit</u>. I will resist him and his influence At All Times.

Principle #3...<u>I Have Authority Over Evil Spirits</u>. They Were Defeated By Jesus And Now I Must Obey My Commands.

Principle #4...<u>I Will Allow The Peace of God To Be My Referee</u> In All My decisions And Life Experiences.

Principle #5...<u>Confusion Is Not of God</u>. When I Am Confused, I Will Stop All Decision-Making Activity And Seek The Lord For His Peace And Wisdom.

Principle #6...I Will Not Be Afraid Because <u>Fear Is Not</u>

From My Heavenly Father. I Can And Will Overcome Those Things That Frighten Me.

Principle #7... All Things Will Work Together For My Good. I Reverence God And Have Been Called By God According To His Purposes. That Qualifies Me For This Promise.

Principle # 8... There Must Be A Reason For That. I Will Not Let Situations That Are Beyond My Control Frustrate Me Or Get Me Angry.

Principle #9... Jesus Is Coming Soon. He Will Set Everything In Order And Rid This World of Evil. I Will Look For His Return And I Will Be Ready.

Principle #10... God's Angels Will Protect Me, therefore *I Can Relax And Feel Safe, Even Though Times Are Getting Worse.*

Your words have power.
Use them to energize your future, stabilize
your NOW and overcome your past.

CHAPTER EIGHT

Prove It To Yourself

The Bible is full of promises from God to His children. They speak of many things from healing to deliverance, salvation, forgiveness and a lot more. The Lord showed me many years ago that these precious promises are really spiritual batteries that His children can use to activate their faith.

If I have a battery, or promise, and I hook up my faith to it, it forms a lifeline that holds me and keeps me in times of trouble. For example: The devil seeks to deceive me into thinking that I am not loved. He brings around folks that criticize me, put me down and laugh at me. Like anyone else, I begin feeling down and worthless. Then I read,

"To the praise of the glory of his grace, wherein he hath made us accepted in the beloved." **Hebrews 1:6**

Suddenly I realize that God has freely given us grace but more than that, He gave it to the ones He loves. I now know that God really loves me and what all those other folks are saying are lies.

I hang my faith on the fact that He loves me and no other voice counts…thus I gain self-respect and self-worth. This is victorious living.

We will be looking at several batteries to hook up to and how to hang our faith on them to overcome the attacks of the enemy and inward self-generated fears.

It is important to realize that there is a real devil that rules over principalities, rulers of darkness and Spiritual wickedness.

"For we wrestle not against flesh and blood, but against principalities, against powers, against the rulers of the darkness of this world, against spiritual wickedness in high places." **Ephesians 6:12**

We are in a situation where we are being attacked every day. There is no neutral ground or safe city. We either fight back or fall prey to deception, lies and oppression. This is not a new concept or doctrine.

Hear what Peter said to the 1st century Christians,

"Be sober, be vigilant; because your adversary, the devil, walks about like a roaring lion, seeking whom he may devour. Resist him, steadfast in the faith, knowing that the same sufferings are experienced by your brotherhood in the world." **I Peter 5:8-9**

It's time to own up to the reality of a real enemy and learn how to fight back. We have precious promises in the Bible that guarantee victory over the sinister forces of evil. It's time to take back what we've lost and declare our freedom from future attacks.

Hooks To Hang Your Faith On

As I have already mentioned, the hook is a Bible verse that is lodged in your mind. It got there from you reading the Bible and seeing the Divine Truth. It was so powerful that you could not help but remember it.

"Thy word have I hid in mine heart, that I might not sin against thee." **Psalm 119:11**

It is our love for God that drives us to hid His Word in our hearts. We may not remember the address of the verse or the exact wording but we do remember the essence of what is being said. This is how a hook comes to be in our mind.

A hook is a promise that God gave to His children. There are over 7,000 in the scriptures. Let's look at a few and see how they apply to our daily life.

Here's a hook that will bring you a clear perspective of life and keep you focused on the things that really matter.

But he answered and said,

"It is written, Man shall not live by bread alone, but by every word that proceeds out of the mouth of God." **Matthew 4:4**

There are many voices out there that call to us, telling us what to think, what to do and how we should live life. The liberal minded speak loudly as to immoral practices and lifestyles. Others push a political agenda that is far from the truth of God's calling.

Everybody we meet has an opinion as to what to wear, do or think. However, Jesus put it into perspective for us when He said we were to live by every word that comes out of the mouth of God.

God's Word clarifies and delineates. It sorts through all the voices and lights up those that speak the truth. We can hook our faith on God's Word, knowing that it will bring peace of mind, clarity of purpose and focus to our thoughts.

To live by the word is to hold up every thought, every voice, and every so-called truth to what the Word says to see how they fare.

If they are not in line with the Word, they are false and can immediately be discarded as error, lies and deception. Thus we walk in the Spirit from Bible truth to Bible truth.

By using God's Word as a clarifying force, we can quickly identify many of the deceptions that other folks have fallen into. All we have to do is say, "What does God's Word say on the subject?" Then look for what has been said. This is what Jesus did in Matthew 4:4. He said, **"It is written"**. He had to have asked himself, what has been said before about this matter. He had already hidden the Word in His heart and could easily find it again when it was needed.

Now let's apply this simple process of holding everything in light of what God has already said on the matter to a few popular beliefs floating in our society today. What does God's Word say?

Reincarnation... *"And as it is appointed unto men once to die, but after this the judgment:"* **Hebrews 9:27**

Once To Die but never over and over again.

Same Sex Marriage...The Bible clearly condemns homosexuality as a sin. Christians that seriously follow God's Word must also condemn it. Listen to what the scriptures say.

Leviticus 20:23...If a man also lie with mankind, as he lies with a woman, both of them have committed an abomination: they shall surely be put to death; their blood shall be upon them.

I Corinthians 6:9-10...*Do you not know that the unrighteous will not inherit the kingdom of God? Do not be deceived. Neither fornicators, nor idolaters, nor adulterers, nor homosexuals, nor sodomites, nor thieves, nor covetous, nor drunkards, nor revilers, nor extortioners will inherit the kingdom of God.*

Romans 1:26-28...*For this cause God gave them up unto vile affections: for even their women did change the natural use into that which is against nature: and likewise also the men, leaving the natural use of the woman, burned in their lust one toward another; men with men working that which is unseemly, and receiving in themselves that recompence of their error which was meet... and even as they did not like to retain God in their knowledge, God gave them over to a reprobate mind, to do those things which are not convenient;*

Sex Before Marriage... *Fornicators shall not inherit the kingdom of God.* **I Corinthians 6:9**

Fornication refers to sexual activity outside of the marriage relationship between a man and a woman. It would include premarital as well as extramarital sexual relationships of whatever duration from a one-night stand to an ongoing affair. Such activity was rampant in first century at Corinth.

It is rampant today in our own society. But it matters not how commonly it is practiced, it is still unrighteous and it will keep one from entering heaven. *Christian Apologetics & Research Ministry*

Abortion ... There are numerous teachings in Scripture that make it abundantly clear what God's view of abortion is. **Jeremiah 1:5** tells us that God knows us before He forms us in the womb. **Psalm 139:13-16** speaks of God's active role in our creation and formation in the womb.

Exodus 21:22-25 prescribes the same penalty—death—for someone who causes the death of a baby in the womb as for someone who commits murder. This clearly indicates that God considers a baby in the womb to be as human as a full-grown adult. For the Christian, abortion is not a matter of a woman's right to choose.

It is a matter of the life or death of a human being made in God's image **(Genesis 1:26-27; 9:6).**

Pornography… Even though the Bible does not say anything about pornography, it is still wrong. Pornography deals with photography and/or illicit paintings and/or cartoons that are designed to arouse sexual passions in the viewer. Nevertheless, we can derive an accurate conclusion from Scriptures that deal with other issues and apply them to the issue of pornography. We are instructed to think of good things not imorral things. Philippians 4:8

"Finally, brethren, whatsoever things are true, whatsoever things are honest, whatsoever things are just, whatsoever things are pure, whatsoever things are lovely, whatsoever things are of good report; if there be any virtue, and if there be any praise, think on these things."

Adultery…Matthew 5:27-28 "You have heard that it was said,

"You shall not commit adultery'; but I say to you, that everyone who looks on a woman to lust for her has committed adultery with her already in his heart."

The Bible tells us to be sexually pure. Matthew recorded Jesus saying if a man looks upon a woman to lust, he has already committed adultery, even though he did not participate in the physical act. Adultery begins in the thoughts of man and can play out in real time if left to fester and grow.

Prostitution… **Lev. 19:29** *"Do not profane your daughter by making her a harlot, so that the land will not fall to harlotry and the land become full of lewdness."*

Deuteronomy 23:17-18 *"None of the daughters of Israel shall be a cult prostitute, nor shall any of the sons of Israel be a cult*

prostitute." "You shall not bring the hire of a harlot or the wages of a dog into the house of the LORD your God for any votive offering, for both of these are an abomination to the LORD your God."

Judgment Day Will Come

Rape, Murder, Burglary, Adultery and Violence of any kind…are all included in immorality, which is not of God. The Bible is full of scripture passages that condemn them and declare their punishment in the final Day of God's judgment. It's not ok to cheat on your spouse, steal from your workplace, take a human life and violate a woman sexually. Those who do will face God's wrath one day and it won't be pretty.

All these things, when held up to the light of the scriptures, are clearly wrong and definitely not God's will for His children. Once we see that, we can stand in opposition to them and avoid the snare of the devil that has captured so many of our fellow believers.

Only One Way To Heaven… Another hook to hang your faith on is *Acts 4:12*, the "One Way" theological truth. *"Neither is there salvation in any other: for there is none other name under heaven given among men, whereby we must be saved."* **Acts 4:12**

Jesus said, as recorded in the gospel of John, *"Thomas saith unto him, Lord, we know not whither thou goest; and how can we know the way? Jesus saith unto him, I am the way, the truth, and the life: no man cometh unto the Father, but by me."* **John 14:6**

We know that the way to heaven is through Jesus and only Him. Being a good person or believing in the church doctrines that promote religion, as a way to salvation will not get you to heaven.

Jesus is the only way to God, the Father. Our destiny, hope of eternal life and very existence is in Him. To believe otherwise is error. Knowing this truth puts us in touch with God and full access to His grace and blessings.

When we believe in Him as the only begotten Son of God that was sent as God's spotless lamb to be sacrificed on Calvary's cross for our sin, we find peace with God and realize the abundant life that Jesus promised. (John 3:16, John 14:6 & John 10:10)

It is hard for most folks that are not "Born Again" to understand why there is just one way to God, yet it is true. There is only one way and that is through Jesus Christ. The Bible is our source to prove that the one-way doctrine is valid. Acts 4:12 is a clear teaching of this doctrine. **NO Other Name**

All the world religions cannot save us. Joining a church or specific faith cannot save us. It must be an acknowledgment of our sin, our cry before the throne of God for forgiveness, and our invitation for Jesus to come into our hearts and save us. His name is the only one that can get us through death into eternal life.

Here are a few scriptures that support the only "One-Way" doctrine.

"There is one God, and one mediator between God and men, the man Christ Jesus; Who gave himself a ransom for all, to be testified in due time." (I Timothy 2:5-6)

"Believe on the Lord Jesus Christ and thou shalt be saved"... (Acts 16:31)

"That if thou shalt confess with thy mouth the Lord Jesus, and shalt believe in thine heart that God hath raised him from the dead, THOU SHALT BE SAVED. For with the heart man be-

lieveth unto righteousness; and with the mouth confession is made unto salvation." (Romans 10:9-10)

The skeptic would say, "You mean to tell me that all the religions of the world are wrong and only Christianity is the one true religion?" Remember, Christianity is not a religion. It is a relationship born out of love between man and the one true and living God.

There is no one true religion. Religion, in itself, will not get us to God. It is the blood of Christ that unlocks the door and our confession of faith in Jesus that makes it all happen. (John 14:6)

Why is Jesus the only way to God? He is the only way because God planned it that way. He set the penalty for sin, which was death.

"The soul that sinneth, it shall die." (Ezekiel 18:20) In fact, Jesus was the slain Lamb of God before the foundation of the world. (Ephesians 1:3-7)

Christianity states that the God of the Bible is the only true God and salvation is only possible by accepting Jesus Christ, His only begotten Son as Savior and Lord. II Corinthians 5:21 says,

"For he hath made him to be sin for us, who knew no sin; that we might be made the righteousness of God in him."

God validated His Son as the only way in multiple ways so we can be assured that Jesus was indeed the only way to Him. Here are some to consider.

Eyewitnesses saw Jesus' miracles and validated them as authentic. Over 500 followers saw Jesus, after His resurrection, and watched Him ascend into heaven.

The prophets foretold of His coming, where He would be born, that He would be God in human flesh and lots more…all prophetic statements were realized in Jesus, even those like in Isaiah chapter 53 that were uttered hundreds of years before Jesus came.

God Himself validated Jesus as His sole pathway to Him. "While he was still speaking, behold, a bright cloud overshadowed them; and suddenly a voice came out of the cloud, saying, *"This is My beloved Son, in whom I am well pleased. Hear ye Him!"* **(Mathew 17:5)**

The Apostles lost their homes, wealth, and even their lives preaching the gospel. Would they do that if it were a lie? I don't think so. They testified to the truth and were willing to die for it if necessary. (See Foxes Book of Martyrs)

Thousands of Believers, over more than twenty centuries have testified of how Jesus helped them and blessed them.

I can personally testify that I have seen the hand of the Lord in my life and communicate with Him daily. I know He is the Christ.

The provability that one man could fulfill all prophecies about a Messiah that God Himself said would come, (Gen.3: 15), and perform fantastic miracles while here on earth, and be raised from the dead, and ascend into heaven while hundreds looked on is astronomical.

But Jesus did just that…fulfilled everything that was foretold about the coming Messiah. He had to be who He said He was and therefore is truly the only way to God.

Now that you know all this, you can draw strength from the truth and believe in Him. It's time to hook your faith on Jesus.

The Witness of The Spirit… As mentioned previously, another hook Is Romans 8:16-17…

"The Spirit Himself bears witness with our spirit that we are children of God, and if children, then heirs—heirs of God and joint heirs with Christ, if indeed we suffer with Him, that we may also be glorified together."

The central truth of Romans 8:16 is that God's Spirit bears witness with our spirit that we are children of God. We don't have to wonder if we are saved or if there is a God or feel like we are all alone in this world.

As we seek the Lord, pray to the Father and ask for guidance, it is the Spirit that communicates with us, telling us what to do, when to do it and how to act.

He actually teaches our hands to war against evil forces. Over a period of time we will develop a history of things that the Spirit has done in our lives. It is this history that becomes the hook for us to hang our faith on.

I can go back in my Christian experience with God, now more than 60 years, and see the hand of the Lord in action on my behalf. It is the Spirit that moves in my favor. If He was there then, there is no reason why He will not show up when I need Him again. Jesus said, I will not leave you comfortless: I will come to you." John 14:18

"But the Comforter, which is the Holy Ghost, whom the Father will send in my name, he shall teach you all things, and bring all things to your remembrance, whatsoever I have said unto you." John 14:26

It is important to listen for the voice of the Spirit. He will confirm your birthright, destiny and resting place. He will walk beside you through every trial and heartache providing wisdom, peace, deliverance, and any other emotional or physical necessity.

Knowing that we are heirs of God and joint heirs with Christ is a powerful position to be in. It is worth all the suffering we may encounter as we serve the Lord. This perspective gives us automatic victory over fear, doubt, worry, and the fiery darts of our enemies.

All Things Work Together... Another hook Is Romans 8:28. We have discussed this one before.

"And we know that all things work together for good to them that love God, to them who are the called according to his purpose."

Here is a hook that is sure to work every time. It is, however, predicated on two things: 1.) You must love God. 2.) you must be in the "Them" crowd who are called according to His purposes.

All," Born Again" folks are in the, "Them" crowd. They make up the church. They are the "Whosoevers" of **John 3:16** that believe that Jesus is the Son of God.

All, "Born Again" believers love God. We actually worship Him and adore Him because He first loved us and gave His only Son as a ransom for our souls.

So, do you qualify? If you do, you can rest assured that all things will work together for your good. It may seem like they don't but you do not see the overall picture as God does.

He knows the beginning from the end and how to operate around man's free will to cause everything to work out in accordance to His will and in our favor.

We have a clear perspective in Romans 8:28. There can be no doubt. What we are experiencing, good or bad, will ultimately work together for our good. Thus we can rest when we go through trials and experience tragedies and suffer loss. God is for us and is actively engaged in keeping us in His will and on the right path to Glory.

"There's a reason for that"…. Hang your faith on this hook and you will find peace of mind, hope, a positive outlook on life and a deeper relationship with your Savor. I use a phrase when things happen. It reminds me of Romans 8:28 and that I should hook my faith upon it. The phrase is ***"There's a reason for that."***

I have taken just a few of the bible verses that are special to me to show you how the scriptures can be hooks to hang your faith on. There are many more promises, biblical truths and treasures to be found in God's Holy Word. It's now up to you to search them out and make them a hook for your faith. I would suggest you read my other Book, **"The Believer's Handbook of Battle Strategies"**. (www.christianliferesourcecenter.org).

Remember, the times in which we live are full of terrorist attacks, fiery darts from the devil, critical judgments of us by others for being conservative, and attitudes of hate from the children of darkness.

We must stand in faith, walk by faith and live in faith to overcome. Knowing the scriptures and believing them with all our hearts can easily accomplish all of this and more.

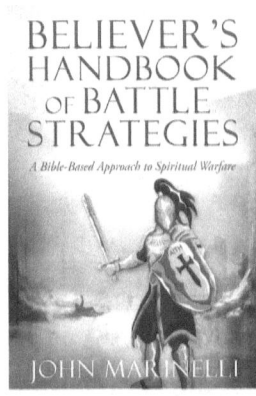

CHAPTER NINE

Manna From Heaven

Living a victorious Christian life requires spiritual food. God rained down Manna from heaven to feed the children of Israel while they were in route from Egypt to the land of Canaan. This was just after God opened the Red sea and the Jews crossed over to safety on dry land.

Their 400+ years in bondage was over and they were heading to posses the "Promised Land" that God gave Abraham. They gave up the fleshpots, cool water and abundance of food, trusting God to provide for them as they entered and traveled through the wilderness.

It is believed that there were over 2 1/2 million in the caravan that Moses led out of Egypt. This would include men, women and children. They all left Egypt with hope, faith, and trust in God and were strongly committed to holding on until they made it to their Promised Land.

> *"And they took their journey from Elim, and all the congregation of the children of Israel came unto the wilderness of Sin, which is between Elim and Sinai, on the fifteenth day of the second month after their departing out*

of the land of Egypt. And the whole congregation of the children of Israel murmured against Moses and Aaron in the wilderness:

And the children of Israel said unto them, Would to God we had died by the hand of the Lord in the land of Egypt, when we sat by the flesh pots, and when we did eat bread to the full; for ye have brought us forth into this wilderness, to kill this whole assembly with hunger.

Manna From Heaven

Then said the Lord unto Moses, Behold, I will rain bread from heaven for you; and the people shall go out and gather a certain rate every day, that I may prove them, whether they will walk in my law, or no.

And it shall come to pass, that on the sixth day they shall prepare that which they bring in; and it shall be twice as much as they gather daily. And Moses and Aaron said unto all the children of Israel, At even, then ye shall know that the Lord hath brought you out from the land of Egypt:" **Exodus 16:1-6**

This Manna was not only God's provision to keep the people alive but it was also a sign that proved that God was really leading them. It was a miracle that would show the Israelites God's love and mercy.

God made sure that the Manna was seen as an authentic miracle by raining it down from heaven. He did this for 40 years.

Manna looked like coriander seed and tasted like wafers made with honey (Exodus 16: 31). When the Israelites saw it, they asked each other, "What is it?" (Heb. man hu [aWh'm]). This led to the name "manna, " "what?"

It came each morning, except on the Sabbath day. It could be collected each day for that day alone, and only as much as could be eaten in one day. If a person tried to collect more than needed or to store the manna for future needs, it would grow wormy and foul (v. 20).

In this way it was impossible for the Israelites to evade total dependence on God or to use the manna greedily for personal gain. Miraculously, the manna could be preserved on the sixth day and eaten on the Sabbath, and it was not to be found on the Sabbath morning (vv. 22-29).

The Rebellious

Eventually, some rebellious Israelites grew tired of the manna and regretted the day they were delivered from their bondage (Num 11:6). They came to detest the manna and longed instead for the rich foods of Egypt (v. 5).

But God continued to give the Israelites a steady supply of manna during their forty years of desert wanderings. When Joshua and the children of Israel crossed the Jordan River and entered the Promised Land at Gilgal, they celebrated the Passover and ate the produce of the land. On that day, the manna ceased, again illustrating its miraculous provision (Joshua 5:12).

The Purpose of The Manna

The purpose of the Manna was to test Israel's faith, to humble them, and to teach them that "Man does not live by bread alone but by every word that comes from the mouth of the Lord" (Deut 8:3,16).

Jesus used this quote to refuse Satan's suggestion that he turn stones into bread (Matt 4:4). Like the Israelites in the desert, Jesus was totally dependent on the provisions of his heavenly Father while in the wilderness of temptation (Matt 4:11).

"Bread of Life" A Metaphor of Jesus

The people in Jesus' day misunderstood the significance of the manna. They longed for a physical miracle, like the manna, which would prove to them that Jesus' words were true (John 6:31). But Jesus wanted his disciples to seek for the bread of heaven that gives life to the world, instead of physical bread to satisfy their appetites. When they asked, give us this bread, he answered, *"I am the bread of life"* (vv. 32-35).

To the church in Pergamos, Jesus encouraged faithfulness by promising that true believers would receive "hidden manna" to eat (Rev 2:17). Just as Moses' manna brought with it physical blessing, so this heavenly reward will bring eternal life. (Contributed by William T. Arnold...Baker's Evangelical Dictionary).

Manna Was The, "Bread of Heaven"

Manna was the "Bread of Heaven" it was a metaphor or picture of Jesus. He said this about Himself.

"I am the Bread of Life" (John 6:35) this is one of the seven "I AM" statements of Jesus.

Jesus used the same phrase *"I AM"* in seven declarations about

Himself. In all seven, He combines "I AM" with tremendous metaphors, which expressed His, saving relationship toward the world. All appear in the book of John.

John 6:35 says, *"I am the bread of life; whoever comes to me shall not hunger, and whoever believes in me shall never thirst."*

A Basic Dietary Item

Bread is considered a staple food—i.e., a basic dietary item. A person can survive a long time on only bread and water. Bread is such a basic food item that it becomes synonymous for food in general. We even use the phrase *"breaking bread together"* to indicate the sharing of a meal with someone.

Bread also plays an integral part of the Jewish Passover meal. The Jews were to eat unleavened bread during the Passover feast and then for seven days following as a celebration of the exodus from Egypt.

Finally, when the Jews were wandering in the desert for 40 years, God rained down *"bread from heaven"* to sustain the nation (Exodus 16:4).

All of this plays into the scene being described in John 6 when Jesus used the term *"bread of life."* He was trying to get away from the crowds to no avail. He had crossed the Sea of Galilee, and the crowd followed Him.

After some time, Jesus inquires of Philip how they're going to feed the crowd. Philip's answer displays his "little faith" when he says they don't have enough money to give each of them the smallest morsel of food.

Finally, Andrew brings to Jesus a boy who had five small loaves of bread and two fish. With that amount, Jesus miraculously fed the people with lots of food to spare.

Afterward, Jesus and His disciples cross back to the other side of Galilee. When the crowd sees that Jesus has left, they follow Him again.

Jesus takes this moment to teach them a lesson. He accuses the crowd of ignoring His miraculous signs and only following Him for the "free meal." Jesus tells them in John 6:27,

"Do not labor for the food that perishes, but for the food that endures to eternal life, which the Son of Man will give to you. For on him God the Father has set his seal."

In Other Words

In other words, they were so enthralled with the food, they were missing out on the fact that their Messiah had come. So the Jews ask Jesus for a sign that He was sent from God (as if the miraculous feeding and the walking across the water weren't enough).

They tell Jesus that God gave them manna during the desert wandering. Jesus responds by telling them that they need to ask for the true bread from heaven that gives life. When they ask Jesus for this bread, Jesus startles them by saying,

"I am the bread of life; whoever comes to me shall not hunger, and whoever believes in me shall never thirst."

A Phenomenal Statement!

This is a phenomenal statement! First, by equating Himself with bread, Jesus is saying he is *essential* for life. Second, the life Jesus is referring to is not physical life, but eternal life. Jesus is trying to get the Jews thinking beyond the physical realm and into the spiritual realm.

He is contrasting what He brings as their Messiah with the bread He miraculously created the day before. That was physical bread that perishes. He is spiritual bread that brings eternal life.

Third, and very important, Jesus is making another claim to deity. This statement is the first of the "I AM" statements in John's Gospel.

The Phrase "I AM"

The phrase "I AM" is the covenant name of God (Yahweh, or YHWH), revealed to Moses at the burning bush (Exodus 3:14). The phrase speaks of self-sufficient existence (or what theologians refer to as *"aseity"*), which is an attribute only God possesses. It is also a phrase the Jews who were listening would have automatically understood as a claim to deity.

Fourth, notice the words "come" and "believe." This is an invitation for those listening to place their faith in Jesus as the Messiah and Son of God.

The Invitation

This invitation to come is found throughout John's Gospel. Coming to Jesus involves making a choice to forsake the world and follow Him. Believing in Jesus means placing our faith in Him that He is who He says He is, that He will do what He says He will do, and that He is the only one who can.

Fifth, there are the words "hunger and thirst." Again, it must be noted that Jesus isn't talking about alleviating physical hunger and thirst.

The key is found in another statement Jesus made, back in His Sermon on the Mount. In Matthew 5:6, Jesus says,

"Blessed are those who hunger and thirst for righteousness, for they shall be satisfied."

When Jesus says those who come to Him will never hunger and those who believe in Him will never thirst, He is saying He will satisfy their hunger and thirst to be made righteous in the sight of God.

Modern Day Use of Manna
A Spiritual Application

Jesus said He was the *"Bread of Life"* and the "Bread" the came down from heaven. We know from John chapter one that Jesus was pre-existent as God and became man so He could be our Savior. Thus the, *"Bread of Heaven"* was and is the Word that became flesh and dwelt among us.

If we go to the Word of God every day, like the Old Testament saints went out to gather Manna, we would be filled with all the spiritual nutrients necessary to live in the wilderness of this world.

The Bible is the Manna of our day. It took hundreds of years to grow and it is for everyone. We need only to open the Bible and gather the spiritual food (Bread) that God has waiting for us.

Never Too Much

I know that some will say, just like the Israelites in the wilderness, I am tired of this Manna. The literal Manna may have become unappealing after eating it for 40 years. However, the *"Bread from heaven"* does not get old; does not loose its flavor and will not cause you to wish for something else that is more satisfying.

The *"Heavenly Manna"* is the word of God and when it is sent from heaven it accomplishes all that God intended it to do.

"So shall my word be that goes forth out of my mouth: it shall not return unto me void, but it shall accomplish that which I please, and it shall prosper in the thing whereto I sent it." Isaiah 545:11

We can trust that when God sends us Manna from heaven, it will arrive safely and be a blessing to us.

The provision of Manna was to sustain the children of God while traveling in the wilderness. The trip was only about 3 1/2 days. However, because of the rebellion and idol worship in the camp, God chose to keep them in a state of wandering for 40 years until a new generation could emerge.

The new generation, at the direction of God, went into the Promised Land and took it for themselves. Once they settled and were able to grow their own food, the Manna stopped falling from heaven. This suggests several things that can apply to the Christian walk for faith. They are:

- The Manna was only temporary. It was never given as a 40-year provision. It ended up being just that but it was not planned that way.
- The purpose of the Manna was to teach faith and dependency to the newly founded nation. It was a way to test their faith on an on-going basis.
- Manna from heaven is a metaphor for Spiritual sustenance but it cannot go beyond the physical realm… whereas the *"Bread of Life"* is an eternal provision.
- The Manna was a sign from God that proved to the people that God was really leading them.

The wilderness is a place of wandering for those that reject God's love and guidance. The rebellious go into it but never come out.

We, like Old Testament saints, have seen the promises of God afar off and now consider ourselves strangers and pilgrims in the earth. Hebrews 11:13… We too are on our way to the Promised Land.

The, *"Bread of Life"* being a type of Spiritual Manna, is designed to sustain us in a wilderness-world as we walk in the Spirit; fight the good fight of faith and stand fast in the liberty that we have in Christ…until we see Jesus face to face and are welcomed home by God, our Heavenly Father.

When that happens, the need for Manna will be no longer because we will have arrived at our destination.

The Bible is the Manna of our day. We will starve and even live life in a weaken state of mind without it. It is our only source by which we can mature in Christ. It is the Manna that helps us to discover the promises of God, and commune with the Holy Spirit.

"Thy word have I hid in mine heart, that I might not sin against thee." Psalm 119:11

CHAPTER TEN

Seeing The Hand of God

Has anyone ever questioned your faith? I had an experience in my early Christian walk where a guy that was not a Christian challenged me as to the validity of my belief in God. He said that God was "Man-Made" and therefore unable to save, heal or anything else. It was his belief that fate drove human life, not God's love and power.

When sickness came knocking at my door, the guy would say, "So, where's your Christianity now?" "If your God is all-powerful, why doesn't He heal you? When I lost my Job, he again said, "So, where's your God; can't your God do anything?

I was a brand new Christian and not very knowledgeable. I didn't have answers for him then. Now, after 60 years of walking with the Lord, I know a few things.... mainly that God does things His way and in His timing.

Fate has no power. Things just don't happen without a reason, even if we do not understand why. God is a Just God. He is the epitome of Love and Righteousness. Even though we go through difficulties, He is still there beside us to comfort us and deliver us from the calamities of life.

How many know that friends do not angrily say, *"Where Is Your God?"* It is the job of your enemy to say such a thing. That enemy wants you dead. If that can't happen, he will go for confusion, backsliding and a faith failure if at all possible, anything to cause you to turn against God.

This strategy has been the key tool of Satan for centuries because it is a lie that is aimed at the less informed and can shake their foundation to the core.

The psalmist wrote in Psalm 42 about his enemies. They attacked him with the same strategy, *"Where IS Your God"* The verses of this psalm tell a story of a man that is overwhelmed, frustrated and confused but not in utter despair. His faith did not fail. It kept him through the storm, even though he didn't know why he suffered so.

Let's look at his life situation. If we look closely, we can see God in the life of a believer and learn how to deal with difficult circumstances.

The God Seeker

The writer of the psalm was not your average believer that seeks spiritual things on Sunday and only at church. He was a God seeker. Read psalm 42 about his lifestyle and see if it fits yours.

"As the hart pants after the water brooks, so pants my soul after thee, O God. My soul thirsts for God, for the living God: when shall I come and appear before God?" Psalm 42:1-2

When your relationship with God turns into a mere religion, you loose that hunger and thirst and slowly but surely stop seeking God. Then you fall away from the quest for real truth and cease from exercising faith. Is that happening to you? I hope not.

We need to be "God Seekers" that long for and seek after the presence of the Lord. We cannot live without it. We should continually ask for it and seek after it. God is our refuge, our shield, our strength, and our very life. We move and life and have our being in Him.

This psalm teaches us that even though we are God Seekers, we can still experience vicious attacks against our faith and trust in God and suffer under cruel accusations from our enemies that are meant to destroy our relationship with God and kill our faith. In other words, we are not exempt because we are the children of God.

Evil At Work
! ! ! Read All About It ! ! !

"My tears have been my meat day and night, while they continually say unto me, **"Where is thy God?"** *I will say unto God my rock, why hast thou forgotten me? Why go I mourning because of the oppression of the enemy? As with a sword in my bones, mine enemies reproach me; while they say daily unto me,* **"Where is thy God?"** Psalms 42:3-9-10

Here's what Jesus said about the enemy and Himself. He compared His goal for mankind with the goals of the devil, known as "The Thief" in Biblical literature.

"The thief cometh not, but for to steal, and to kill, and to destroy: I am come that they might have life, and that they might have it more abundantly." John 10:10

Note that the accusation, *"Where Is Your God"* brought tears to the writer of Psalm 42. The continual mocking by his enemies overwhelmed him. It even caused him to go back to his rock, that being God, where he always found answers and refuge and questioned Him saying,

"Why hast thou forgotten me? Why go I mourning because of the oppression of the enemy?"

In today's language expression, we would probably say, "Why Me Lord." "What did I do wrong that you should stop protecting me from my enemies? He is feeling sadness. He is actually mourning over his situation. His focus has been shifted to himself instead of God where he once drew all of his strength and well-being.

Question? Why does he care about what his enemies think? So what if they continually mock his God. Hasn't the psalmist had enough encounters with God to know He would never really forsake him? Unless, he is beginning to believe that God really has forgotten him. This is what the psalmist is indeed thinking…a lie of the devil that is like a fiery dart that, if allowed into the soul, will kill, steal and destroy.

The Recovery

We all go through tough times and experience ridicule and even mocking from those that reject our Savior and our faith. You know how I know that's true?

"Yea, and all that will live godly in Christ Jesus shall suffer persecution." II Timothy 3:12

It's not what happens to us that alters our thinking or keeps us from walking with the Lord. It is rather how we react to what has happened that defeats us or brings us into victory and peace. See how the Psalmist deals with his situation.

He remembers the past, when he was so happy with the Lord; he rebukes his own soul for being cast down; and he makes an incredible statement of faith right in the face of his oppressors.

"When I remember these things, I pour out my soul in me: for I had gone with the multitude, I went with them to the house of God, with the voice of joy and praise, with a multitude that kept holyday.

Why art thou cast down, O my soul? And why art thou disquieted in me? Hope thou in God: for I shall yet praise him for the help of his countenance." **Psalm 42:4-5**

Note: The Psalmist has not as yet learned why God has not been there for him. He is still sad about not knowing and the continual mocking from his enemies is getting to him, yet he puts his trust in God anyway. His trust is based upon past experiences where God was there and he was delivered.

Though he did not understand, it didn't mean that God wasn't working things out and has a good reason for what He is doing. This is not blind faith but rather faith based upon past experience.

If you are in a similar situation, there is no need to blame God… that is, if you know that He is a loving, kind, longsuffering and a caring God who has your best interest at heart. God just doesn't bring evil our way.

Sometimes God will share His reasoning for what He does in our lives. Sometimes He won't.

You'll remember Job and all he went through. He too cried out for an audience with God and had people telling him to repent and even curse God, yet he held off from blaming God and in the end never did find out why all those thing fell upon him.

Again, it is not what happens to you but how you react to what happens that defeats you or delivers you.

Pray, Pray and Pray Some More

When we are cast down, we are somewhat incapacitated. We don't want to think, sometimes eat or even work. Being cast down is otherwise known as "Depression" and it's a killer if not overcome. It creates a feeling of being overwhelmed. You loose interest in life and your countenance shifts from happy to sad.

All of this was happening to the Psalmist. He was feeling all of this and probably even more. Could it be that all of this "Down" is a results of believing a lie that was drilled into him by his enemies?

"Where Is Your God" brings up additional questions and statements that are inferred in the original accusation. Statements like:

1. If you cannot see or feel God, Is He real?

2. If God is silent, does that mean He doesn't care?

3. If God doesn't meet my timing, am I less important than others?

4. If I do not see the hand of God, does it exist?

5. If God doesn't come to my rescue, is He all-powerful?

Because He is not acting like a bellhop tied to your every whim doesn't mean He isn't real or care or all-powerful. It only suggests that He is God and not you.

Remember, with God, there is no finality unless He says so. He can raise you from the dead. He can cause old dry bones to live again. He can heal even after doctors give up. He is God and there is none beside Him.

Here's what the psalmist did in the midst of his depression.

"O my God, my soul is cast down within me: therefore will I remember thee from the land of Jordan, and of the Hermonites, from the hill Mizar. Deep calls unto deep at the noise of thy waterspouts: all thy waves and thy billows are gone over me. Yet the Lord will command his lovingkindness in the day time, and in the night his song shall be with me, and my prayer unto the God of my life." **Psalm 42:6-8**

It sounds to me like the psalmist is saying… "even though I am overwhelmed, sad, depressed and just not with it, I will remember you everywhere I go"

It seems like God has forgotten me but deep within my soul, I know He has not forgotten. In fact, I believe that God will be with me day and night. He will show me His love while I am awake and His song will comfort me as I sleep.

What a powerful declaration of faith. Note that it is based upon past experiences with God. It isn't just blind faith based upon a glimmer of hope.

Self Examination Instruction and Comfort

When there is no one to help in times of trouble and God seems to be occupied somewhere else, what do you do? Some folks just fall apart under the stress. Others buy self-help books and listen to TV talk shows where popular actors give advice. Not so with this psalmist. He speaks directly to his own soul with Godly counsel that probably came to him from God a thousand times before in different situations. Here's what he tells himself.

"Why art thou cast down, O my soul and why art thou disquieted in me? Hope thou in God: for I shall yet praise him for the help of his countenance." Psalm 42:8

His counsel to himself is to chill out, calm down and get back to hoping in God. He tells himself that his future will be bright and that he will once again praise God for the help he needs. He actually calls forth something that does not exist based upon all the other times that it did exist and demonstrates trust in God to be there for him, even though it seems like God is not there now.

How great is that? When we can speak for God based upon what He has done in the past. How great it is that we can also comfort ourselves with our past experiences with God. If He did it then, He'll do it again. I don't know how. I don't know when but He'll do it again because that is who He is.

Now let me ask you the same question that the enemies of the psalmist asked him. **"Where Is Your God?"** Can you honestly say that you know where God is? Will He be there for you in times of trouble? Is He God or not? If He is not all-powerful, He is not God and you are kidding yourself and your faith is in vein.

Christianity is a dynamic relationship with the only true and living God. It is not a religion or a crutch to get you through. You actually do hear the voice of God and see His handiwork in your life. There is a back and forth, not just a one-way communication. He answers prayer and leads us to a divine destiny.

The Bible tells us where God is. That's how we know and why we can put our trust in Him. Here are a few references so you know I am not just making up a story. These are also step-stones in living a good Christian life.

"Let your conversation be without covetousness; and be

content with such things as ye have: for he hath said, I will never leave thee, nor forsake thee." **Hebrews 13:5**

"Be strong and of a good courage, fear not, nor be afraid of them: for the Lord thy God, he it is that doth go with thee; he will not fail thee, nor forsake thee" **Deuteronomy 31:6.**

"I will not leave you comfortless: I ill come to you." **John 14:18**

"Have not I commanded thee? Be strong and of a good courage; be not afraid, neither be thou dismayed: for the Lord thy God is with thee whithersoever thou goest." **Joshua 1:9**

"For I the Lord thy God will hold thy right hand, saying unto thee, Fear not; I will help thee." **Isaiah 41:13**

Yea, though I walk through the valley of the shadow of death, I will fear no evil: for thou art with me; thy rod and thy staff they comfort me." **Psalm 23:4**

"The fear of man brings a snare: but whoso putts his trust in the Lord shall be safe." **Proverbs 29:25**

"For God hath not given us the spirit of fear; but of power, and of love, and of a sound mind." **II Timothy 1:7**

"For ye have not received the spirit of bondage again to fear; but ye have received the Spirit of adoption, whereby we cry, Abba, Father." **Romans 8:15**

"Are not two sparrows sold for a farthing? and one of

them shall not fall on the ground without your Father, but the very hairs of your head are all numbered. Fear ye not therefore, ye are of more value than many sparrows." **Matthew 10:29-31**

"Fear not, little flock; for it is your Father's good pleasure to give you the kingdom." **Luke 12:32**

"And I will pray the Father, and he shall give you another Comforter, that he may abide with you for ever;" **John 14:16**

Do you now understand that God is with you, even if you don't see or feel Him? Your enemy will mock and ridicule you for following Jesus and being a "God Seeker" but that's ok. You want to know why it's ok?

Because, *"If we suffer, we shall also reign with him: if we deny him, he also will deny us:"*

Next time you are challenged to defend God, tell those folks that your God needs no instruction from them. He is doing His own thing and will accomplish all that He has chosen to do.

God is an **All-Powerful God**. That means He is never late. He can reverse anything that has been placed upon us, even after we die. He is the God of Resurrection and we are His children.

"Where Is Your God" If you are a child of God, God is your Heavenly Father and He is by your side at all times to be sure you make it through every calamity in life. His counsel and wisdom is at your disposal. His love and blessings are continually upon you. You are highly favored by God because of what Jesus did.

"Oh how great is thy goodness, which thou hast laid up for them

that fear thee; which thou hast wrought for them that trust in thee before the sons of men!" Psalms 31:19

Don't be afraid to trust Him and praise Him and worship Him in all that you do, even when He seems somewhat aloof. He is still there. Above all…don't give place to the mockers and critics that attack your faith and try to get you to doubt God's love. They will reap what they sow and die in their sins as you walk with the Holy Spirit straight into glory.

CHAPTER ELEVEN

Don't Worry, Be Happy

Everyone wants to be happy. I have never met a person that told me their ambition in life was to be sad. However, many of us, being "Christian Folk", are sad, depressed, and just disappointed with life.

Much of this attitude is because of how life has treated us. Things have not particularly gone the way we imagined. People have let us down. We didn't get the breaks that others seem to get. We seem to have fallen under the stress of daily trials.

Listen to what Helen Keller said so many years ago. You'll remember that she was both deaf and unable to speak until Anne Sullivan taught her sign language. Here's what she said...

"When one door of happiness closes, another opens, but often we look so long at the closed door that we do not see the one that has been opened for us." —**Helen Keller**

I use her quote because it typifies the core problem with those that are not happy. They spend too much time looking at closed doors instead of searching for the open door that God has waiting for them.

Joy - - Pleasure - - Happiness

Psalm 16:11 ...*You will make known to me the path of life; In Your presence is fullness of joy; In Your right hand there are pleasures forever.*

The Bible tells us where to find Joy. It is in the presence of the Lord. His right hand is full of endless pleasure. However, it all comes together when He makes known to us the path of life. It is in His will where we find our destiny, not in the things of this world.

"My brethren, count it all joy when ye fall into divers temptations knowing this, that the trying of your faith works patience. But let patience have her perfect work, that ye may be perfect and entire, wanting nothing." **James 1:2-4**

James tells us that we are to count or consider it pure joy when we experience diverse or various temptations. James explains further by saying it is actually the trying or testing of our faith for the purpose of producing patience. The experience is meant to perfect the believer so they are wanting for nothing.

There is something about patience that sustains us and keeps us from anger, envy, jealousy and all the other works of the flesh that are listed in Galatians chapter five.

Let's Explore

I'd like to explore the concept of various trials, otherwise known as temptations. Let's reason together and see if we can make sense of what James is really saying.

James is talking to believers, not pagans. He is teaching them a,

"How To" truth about dealing with life in a corrupt and sinful world.

He knows that his brethren are or will soon be persecuted for their faith. He doesn't tell them to get into an argument and fight with everybody that ridicules them for being moral, conservative, truthful and a lover of God. He leaves all that stuff up to the individual believer and their walk with God.

What James does say is astounding. He tells them how to deal with the attack from a supernatural, "Walk In The Spirit" perspective.

Point #1....."I'm Falling"

Notice in the scripture that James does not say, "When you are led into various trials". He says, "When you FALL into various trials".

We all try real hard to do the right thing, think the right thoughts and be a good person. However, all of us fall because we are still battling the, "Flesh", the, "Old Man", a "Sinful Nature".

Point #2...Not of God

That means the thing we are experiencing that is a temptation or trial is not of God. He is not responsible for our failures, we are...and that's ok because we are of a fallen race and have not as yet obtained complete salvation.

Yes, we are seated with Christ in heavenly places. Yes, we are more than conquers in Christ. We are indeed forgiven through the Blood of Christ and saved by His Life. What we are not is perfected in the flesh.

Point #3...A New Perspective

So, when we fall, James tells us to laugh it off and focus our attention on a new perspective by considering the trial as a happy occasion...thus, *"Count it all Joy"*. How do you feel about that?

Here you are in the midst of a thing. It could be financial, marital, emotional or otherwise. You are depressed and struggling with it, not sure what to do or how to get away from it. Your focus is on, "It" all the time.

When, "It" dominates your thinking, you have no room for what God wants. In fact, you will find it hard to see into spiritual things or hear the voice of the Lord. That is why James says, *"Count it all Joy"*, because that is the pivot phrase that will open the door to an orderly escape from the temptation.

Point #4...Logical Ascent

Once we shift our thoughts to what God desires for us, we escape the torment for which the trial was intended. We move in a logical ascent from depression, fear, worry and all that other stuff towards a walk of faith.

The trial no longer stands as the primary subject of our thought life. We begin to seek the Lord and find His will.

Yes, we will still be faced with the temptation but instead of a looming giant over us, it is just another attack by evil forces. The mountain thus becomes a molehill.

Point #5...Temptation's Sources

The fact that we fall into temptation is indicative to the trial. It is a setup or snare, designed by Satan to enslave and torment us.

By it's very design, it is meant to keep us from enjoying our Lord and the joy of His fellowship.

There are two main sources of temptation. They are:

The powers of darkness, which include Satan, the devil, evil spirits and the like. They use their fiery darts and snares against us.

The fallen nature, that is in all of us. Its deeds are seen in Galatians chapter five and its ambition is to rule over us. The Bible calls it, **"The Flesh"**. We are admonished to walk in the spirit so as not to fulfill the lust of the flesh.

Point #6...Understanding Life

Some younger or new Christians, when faced with a trial or temptation will cry out to God, Saying, ***"Why Me Lord"***. They are unaware of why things happen and how God uses those things for good in their lives. When we surrender to the Lordship of Christ, we sign a spiritual pledge that Jesus is Lord, not we ourselves. It is His will that we seek and not our own.

So, if a thing enters our day that is not from God but is capable of tempting us to sin, we know not to follow its path. We understand that God's will is supreme and takes priority over our desires. This is understanding the Christian life.

Point #7...The End Result

Romans 8:28 tells us how God responds to what is happening to us. Here's what it says.

"And we know that all things work together for good to them that love God, to them who are the called according to his purpose"

God calls us all according to His divine will or purpose. We love God because He first loved us and saved us from our own sin.

The scripture says if…we love God and are called by Him, He will work everything together for good, even the temptation or trial we have fallen into. The end result is good, not evil. That means the attack is nullified and the damage is repaired so we become more complete in Him.

It Came To Pass

I have noticed a phrase in the Bible that really stands out. It says, **"And It Came To Pass."** Notice that says a lot about a thing…It comes our way but cannot stay. If we reject it, it passes by us and on to someone else.

So it is when we fall into a thing. It knocks at our door on its way, looking to leave a wake of destruction in our souls. Knowing that it will pass and that it is not here forever is a great comfort. It makes it all bearable as we call upon the Lord for our salvation.

The Trying of Your Faith Works Patience

The temptation is used by God to try or test your faith. He did not send the trial your way but does use it never the less.

Is your faith a sustaining faith that will keep you? Are you just pretending when it comes to believing? Can you use your faith to move mountains? God takes advantage of what was meant for evil to show us what is really in our hearts. He wants us to know exactly where we stand…in faith or not.

He also wants to work into us a lasting foundation, made from patience that will endure hardship. If we are patient in dealing with trials, we are stronger in mind and spirit. It means we do not jump to conclusions, cry in desperation and fall apart in the face of temptation. We rather deal in faith according to the will of God. Here's an example of what I mean.

Be sober, be vigilant; because your adversary the devil, as a roaring lion, walks about, seeking whom he may devour: Whom resist stedfast in the faith, knowing that the same afflictions are accomplished in your brethren that are in the world. **I Peter 5:8-9**

A Perfect Work

"But let patience have her perfect work, that ye may be perfect and entire, wanting nothing".

This is a process over time. It grows with every trial taking us from glory to glory.

With each trial comes more patience that brings more peace and a clearer perspective. As we learn to deal with temptations of varying sorts, we grow in grace and faith. This expands our understanding of God, of evil, of life on earth and even eternity. We become more complete in Him having want for nothing.

Wanting For Nothing?

That is correct. There is a point in every Christian's walk with their Lord that the desires of the flesh and the lust of the world begins to fade away. The point is…when we draw closer to Jesus in love and fellowship that all we really desire is more of Him.

The lust for "Stuff" seems silly and the craving for power has no more appeal. We find ourselves at peace with God and comfortable in our own skin. All is well with our souls, even in the midst of ciaos. We become content living in the will of God.

This is why James can say to us, "Count it all Joy' because he knows that the end result, if we allow patience to do its work, is that we will have overcome all the tricks and fiery darts of the devil and the fleshly appetites of sin. We will overcome all of that and walk in the Spirit with a perspective far above those around us.

Stop looking at the door that has been shut and channel your energies on finding the open door that God has for you.

With every trial or temptation there is a way of escape.

"There hath no temptation taken you but such as is common to man: but God is faithful, who will not suffer you to be tempted above that ye are able; but will with the temptation also make a way to escape, that ye may be able to bear it." **I Corinthians 10:13**

Find it and use it. It was made specifically for you.

You are not alone. Others suffer the same trials. (*There hath no temptation taken you but such as is common to man.* **I Corinthians 10:13**)

Resist the devil, knowing he will flee from you.

I Peter 5:8

Walk in the Spirit and you will not be acting out the deeds of the flesh. (*This I say then, Walk in the Spirit, and ye shall not fulfill the lust of the flesh.*) **Galatians 5:16**

Know that no matter what is going down, God will intervene and work it all together for good…If we love Him and are called according to His purposes.

CHAPTER TWELVE

Let God's Peace Rule

We are living in a world that is full of anger, hate and suffering. We face the threats of terrorism, war, unemployment, racial unrest and economic collapse among other things. Finding peace is a lost art because the news keeps telling us all the bad stuff and why we should be afraid or worry.

Today is not that different than when the apostle Paul was on the earth. He lived in a time of economic stress, hate and hard times yet in the midst of all of life's trials, he writes to the fledgling church of the first century,

"And let the peace of God rule in your hearts, to the which also ye are called in one body; and be ye thankful" **Colossians 3:5**

How can one be thankful and remain at peace when another country has invaded yours and now rules with an iron hand? How can peace rule in the hearts of those that are enslaved, ridiculed and degraded? Those were the days of Roman rule.

I can answer these questions with a simple explanation of the scripture given above. But first, here are a few Bible verses to meditate upon.

Psalm 85:8...NIV...*I will listen to what God the LORD says;*

he promises peace to his people, his faithful servants— but to let them not turn to folly.

Phillipians 4:7... *"And the peace of God, which passeth all understanding, shall keep your hearts and minds through Christ Jesus."*

Psalm 29:11... *"The Lord will give strength unto his people; the Lord will bless his people with peace."*

Psalm 119:165... *"Great peace have they which love thy law: and nothing shall offend them."*

John 6:33... *"These things I have spoken unto you, that in me ye might have peace. In the world ye shall have tribulation: but be of good cheer; I have overcome the world."*

I Corinthians 14:33... *"For God is not the author of confusion, but of peace, as in all churches of the saints."*

Psalm 37:37...*"Mark the perfect (Mature) man, and behold the upright: for the end of that man is peace."*

Romans 14:7...*"For the kingdom of God is righteousness and peace and joy in the Holy Spirit."*

Great Trials Bring Great Victories

The psalmist tells us, "many are the afflictions of the righteous, but the LORD delivers us out of them all" **(Psalm 34:19)**.

If you are really serious about walking with God, He will teach you, and guide you, and comfort you, and yes, you will know His peace in your life. In fact, as you mature in your walk with the Lord, peace and joy will be multiplied unto you. It is an interesting paradox that our heavenly Father orchestrates in our lives.

Most pastors will teach that when you are seeking to find God's will, you can identify the leading of the Holy Spirit when you sense God's peace about a matter.

I agree, and I believe that is absolutely true. The peace of God is one of the key indicators of God's guidance.

Colossians 3:15 tells us to *"let the peace of God rule in our hearts."*

Peace is the umpire of our hearts, telling us if we are "safe" in God's will, or "out," following our own path or the deception of the devil.

The prophet Isaiah wrote, *"For you shall go out with joy, and be led out with peace"* **Isaiah 55:12**.

God's best for our lives is that we will be led forth in peace and joy.

The life of the Christian is one of peace and joy. That is why Paul and Silas could sing praises to God in the Philippians jail. **Acts 16:25**

That is why the apostles praised the Lord after being beaten by the teachers of the law, rejoicing that they were counted worthy to suffer shame in Christ's name. **Acts 5:40-41**

That is why Stephen could praise the God of heaven as he was being stoned for his bold witness. **Acts 7:55-60**

Supernatural Peace

There are times, when we are seeking the will of God and we reach the point of decision that we experience supernatural peace. This is an important aspect of discerning between good an evil, and it comes by reason of use **(Hebrews 5:14).**

The peace of God is like a compass for our souls, leading us in the direction that the Holy Spirit intends for our lives. We can take great comfort in knowing that the sovereign God is so involved in our lives that He would supply us with this internal compass as we seek to do His will.

The dictionary Defines The Peace of God This Way

Peace is a state of tranquility or quietness of spirit that transcends circumstances. The term peace is described in Scripture as a gift from God and congruent with His character **(1 Thessalonians 5:23; Galatians 6:16; 1 Peter 1:2; Hebrews 13:20).**

The Bible reveals to us that the foundation of all true peace is a proper relationship with our God and Creator. Ultimate peace is the individual being reconciled to God. (Bibletruth.org) This can only happen through Jesus Christ, His only Begotten Son. **(John 3:16)**

Using The Peace of God As A Referee

Let's take another look at **Colossians 3:15**

"And let the peace of God rule in your hearts, to the which also ye are called in one body; and be ye thankful."

Here is the key to a successful Christian Life. Fail in this exercise and you will never attain peace and will stay frustrated, angrey and depressed all the days of your life.

However, when you apply the scripture, it really works and you can see its affect immediately. Here's what you do:

- Treat the word, "Rule" as a "Referee."
- Listen for the voice of reason.

- Obey what the Holy Spirit tells you to do.
- Stand in faith and hold on to your initial decision.
- Do not waiver in action or thoughts.
- Trust in the Lord that He knows best.
- Reject every thought that tries to change your course of action.

It's All About The Process

When you have peace, it is a gift from God's Holy Spirit. We can walk in it and allow it to rule. This means a total surrender to God's will, knowing that He knows best. Once you are there, your will does not count. It is not a concern anymore.

Your heart and mind are focused to doing God's will and you are decicated to searching it out and doing it. This is what it means to let the "Peace of God" rule.

Now that you are surrendered to doing the will of God, you have to seriously listen for His voice. He will tell you if you are in or out of His will. He uses His Peace to communicate with you.

If you have peace in a situation, you are in His will. This is assuming you have talked it over with God and still feel what you are about to do is right.

If you start loosing His peace, getting confused or feeling skeptical, back away from it because it is leading you out of God's will.

It's like the Holy Spirit is blowing a whistle, like a feferee, and yelling, "Off Sides!" He uses the absence of peace to tell you that you are moving away from the will of God.

So the process is to surrender to God's will, listen for His voice,

Obey what He says, allow His peace to referee, and never move out of its influence.

Walking in the peace of God takes time. We have to learn how because it is not automatic. It's like learning to play the piano. There are the basics, then lots of practice and mistakes, but finally comes the joy of getting it right and doing it. The good thing about it is God wants us to have and enjoy His peace.

No one can take it away from us. We can give it up, the devil can steal it if we are not careful, but it is ours do with or without.

Don't think that anyone can experience the Peace of God. It is not even offered to most people. You must be, "Born Again," to experience the Peace of God.

If you doubt my claim, read **John 3:1-3**. It says, *"There was a man of the Pharisees, named Nicodemus, a ruler of the Jews: The same came to Jesus by night, and said unto him, Rabbi, we know that thou art a teacher come from God: for no man can do these miracles that thou doest, except God be with him. Jesus answered and said unto him, Verily, verily, I say unto thee, except a man be born again, he cannot see the kingdom of God."*

When you are, "Born Again" you become a child of God. Jesus taught Nicodemus this truth in verses 5-6,

"Jesus answered, Verily, verily, I say unto thee, except a man be born of water, (Physical Birth), and of the Spirit, (Spiritual Birth), he cannot enter into the kingdom of God. That which is born of the flesh is flesh; and that which is born of the Spirit is spirit."

So we need to be born of the Spirit in order to see the kingdom of God. Guess what?

"For the kingdom of God is not meat and drink; but righteousness, and peace, and joy in the Holy Ghost" **Romans 14:17**

It's the "Born Again" folks that are given the Spirit who in turn brings "Peace" along with other gifts and fruit into their lives. Thus they gain access to the Peace of God which rules or referee's their everyday.

GOD'S LITTLE TWO BY FOUR

God has a little 2" X 4"
That rest on heaven"s windowsill.
He uses it now and then,
When we stray from His will.

Sometimes we need a good "Bap";
With the Lord"s little 2" X 4"
To knock out the confusion,
And help us to desire Him more.

The Lord"s little 2" X 4"
Is what we sometimes need,
To get our thinking straight,
And keep our focus indeed.

The Lord"s little 2" X 4"
Is fashioned from life"s every trial,
So we do not stray from His will,
Or fall into an ungodly lifestyle.

Written By
John Marinelli

CONCLUSION

Listen to what the apostle told the 1st century Christian church. He said this...

"For I am persuaded, that neither death, nor life, nor angels, nor principalities, nor powers, nor things present, nor things to come, Nor height, nor depth, nor any other creature, shall be able to separate us from the love of God, which is in Christ Jesus our Lord." **Romans 8:38-39**

Paul was persuaded. What persuaded him? Was it not his relationship with the living Christ?

He heard His voice, He studied the scriptures so he had hooks to hang his faith on; He rested in the finished work of Christ, knowing that God was with him; He knew where he came from, why he was born at that time in history and where he was going when his life was over. This is how to live a victorious Christian Life.

Though he had all kinds of resistance to his preaching and even physical attacks, he remained true to his faith and loyal to his relationship with God.

We need to be "Fully persuaded" that God is able and willing to bring about His glorious destiny into our lives. Fully persuaded is what makes our Christianity so meaningful.

I hope you have seen and read enough so that you will give Him His rightful place as Lord.

FRAGILE FLOWER RED

As a flower in earthen sod,
I bloom for thee, oh God.
To blossom with the turn of spring,
to be to you, a beautiful thing.

I lift my Fragile Flower Red
upward from my earthen bed,
to draw light from God above,
strength and peace and joy and love.

As a flower, I bloom for Thee,
that passersby may stop and see.
Your fragrance and beauty I am,
flowered in grace as a man.

As a flower in earthen sod,
I bloom for Thee, oh God.
Upward, I lift my head,
as a Fragile Flower Red.

Written By Rev.
John Marinelli

ABOUT THE AUTHOR

Rev. John Marinelli

Rev. Marinelli is an ordained minister, He has formed and been pastor of one church in Wisconsin and was the pastor of another in Alabama. He has also been a youth minister and evangelism director over the years.

Rev. Marinelli has authored several books including: "Original Story Poems", "The Art of Writing Christian Poetry," "Pulpit Poems," "Moonlight & Mistletoe," "The Mysterious Stranger," "With Eagles Wings," "Mysteries & Miracles," "It Came To Pass," Why Do The Righteous Suffer," and "Believer's Handbook of battle Strategies."

He is also the author of over 80 eBooks on various Christian subjects. The eBooks are all free downloads from his website:

www.christianliferesourcecenter.org

John is an accomplished Christian poet. He also dabbles in songwriting and writing one act Christian plays.

He is the Vice President of Have A Heart For Companion Animals, Inc., a "No Kill" animal welfare organization…

www.haveaheart.us

Rev. Marinelli is now retired from the sales and marketing arena after spending over 40 years in business-to-business and non-profit marketing.

Rev. Marinelli enjoys writing Christian fiction stories, playing chess, singing karaoke and a retired lifestyle in sunny Florida.

For More Info or eMail Communication, Contact
johnmarinelli@embarqmail.com

Really,
This Is The End
Of The Book

The End